BATTLEFIELD

A GLINT
IN THE SKY

BATTLEFIELD BRITAIN

A GLINT
IN THE SKY

MARTIN EASDOWN
with
THOMAS GENTH

Pen & Sword
LOCAL

First published in Great Britain in 2004 by
PEN & SWORD LOCAL
an imprint of
Pen & Sword Books Limited
47 Church Street
Barnsley
South Yorkshire
S70 2AS

Copyright © Martin Easdown and Thomas Genth, 2004

ISBN: 1 84415 119 0

Typeset in 9pt Palatino by Pen & Sword Books Limited

Printed and bound in England by
CPI UK

For a complete list of Pen & Sword titles please contact:
PEN & SWORD BOOKS LIMITED
47 Church Street, Barnsley, South Yorkshire, S70 2AS, England
email: enquiries@pen-and-sword.co.uk • website: www.pen-and-sword.co.uk

Contents

Introduction

While the county of Kent's involvement in the Second World War has been well documented, the air and sea raids suffered by its civilians during the Great War of 1914-1918 have been less so. Indeed, aside from the books and commemorative booklets issued on Dover, Thanet and Folkestone immediately after the ending of the conflict, the raids have never been touched upon in great detail, until now. Being a local, rather than a military, historian has enabled me to concentrate on the effects of the raids on the civilians themselves, rather than the military aspects as covered in previous books on Kent in the First World War. The roles of the Kentish airfields of the RFC and RNAS, and the Dover Patrol, for example, have been covered in great detail in other works and so are not repeated here.

However, I felt it was appropriate that some attention was paid to the German aircraft and Zeppelins and their crews, who brought the war home to the people of the Garden of England. And to counterbalance my understandable bias towards the circumstances of the raids as an Englishman, I felt it would be only fair to include viewpoints from the German side and feature the thoughts of some of their pilots who took part. After all it cannot be denied that they were undoubtedly brave men in choosing to fly those rickety old craft in weather both foul and fair, and it could be argued they were only carrying out orders. Therefore I was extremely fortunate in obtaining assistance in the preparation of this book from Thomas Genth, who has provided interesting details on many aspects of the Gothas and the raids. Thomas's grandfather, Adolf Genth, was an experienced Gotha flyer who took part in the raids on England, and his story, as well as those of the unfortunate victims, is featured herein.

At the heart of the book lies the worst air raid to affect civilians in Kent, and the single greatest tragedy to have befallen the port and seaside town of Folkestone. The disaster occurred on the warm spring evening of Friday, 25 May 1917 when, during the first ever raid on Britain by German Gotha bombers, 78 civilians and 18 military personnel (96 in total) were killed in Folkestone and its neighbourhood, 61 from a single bomb dropped in Tontine Street (the highest civilian death-toll from one bomb during the First World War). After the east coast bombardment of 16 December 1914, this was the greatest civilian tragedy to have hit the home population of Britain up to that point during the war, and thereafter it was to be exceeded only once. I have endeavoured to provide an accurate chronological account of the air raid and clear up some of the previous inaccuracies related to it. For example, the long-held belief that the total number of civilian dead in Folkestone was 71 has been found to be one short, Marie Snoawert, who died of her injuries a month after the raid having not been included in that total. Therefore the memorial plaque in Tontine Street is also wrong; its total of 60 dead also fails to include Miss Snoawert, whose fatal injures were received there. The total number of military dead at Shorncliffe Camp from the raid has proved a problem to researchers in the past and various figures have been given ranging up to 23. Yet after exhaustive research the figure I have arrived at is 18 (17 Canadians and 1 British).

As well as the air raids themselves, I have also touched upon other Kentish war-related civilian tragedies such as the *Princess Irene* and Faversham gunpowder explosions. Key enemy action on the British mainland throughout the war has also been included, though for a fuller account a number of excellent publications may be found in the bibliography.

War, especially when it affects civilians, tends to give a tug on the heartstrings and, having young children myself, the killing of defenceless women and children left a deep impression on me, as perhaps it will for you. Yet for those civilians who died, surely it is only right that they too should be remembered, as were the brave boys of both sides who gave their lives for their country. After reading this book I'm sure you will agree.

Martin Easdown 2004

Acknowledgements

Sincere thanks are due to the following for their assistance in the preparation of this book: Linda Sage, Peter and Anne Bamford, Alan F Taylor, Eamonn Rooney, John T Williams, Shorncliffe Army Camp, Margaret Care, Sandra Francis of Shepway District Council, Susan Hamilton, Jill West, Ann Gaston, Hilary Tolputt, the library staff at Ashford, Deal, Dover, Faversham, Folkestone, Ramsgate, Sheerness and Sittingbourne; the Imperial War Museum, the Folkestone Herald, Anna Rosa Auten, Janice Brooker, Arthur Mattock, Edith Cole, Mrs Gold, Bert Prior, Doris Jones, Rosa Moseley, William Mitchell, E Williams, Lilian 'Cornish' Stanley, Lily Richards, Rose Hayward, Babs Gibbs, Lily Mott, Ellen Edwards, Gladys Willson, Annie Clarke, Joan Holloway, George Turner and Ken Austin.

'Fashionable Folkestone' two years before the outbreak of war. On a warm summer's day the famous Leas Promenade is thronged with its wealthy patrons enjoying the air and listening to the band. Marlinova Collection

Chapter One

ONE GOOD FAVOUR DESERVES ANOTHER

THE GREAT WAR COMES TO FASHIONABLE FOLKESTONE

August 1914 seems almost prehistoric,
So remote that it is difficult to reconstruct the period
Yet the world went very well then.
J C Carlile (1920)

The Great War of 1914-1918 did indeed change the world, especially for the well-off like Mr Carlile, for whom things would never be quite the same again. Before the war Folkestone was one of the most successful and aristocratic seaside resorts in the country, in addition to being a thriving port, and Mr Carlile could not help but look back nostalgically to the golden summer of 1914:

The Folkestone season was opening; thousands of visitors had flocked to the town, attracted by the health-giving qualities of the breezes from the sea and the charm of the scenery. Passengers crossing from the Continent watch for the white cliffs that stand for England. How lovely they are to the eyes of wanderers returning home. They are as welcome as the grasp of friendship. As the ship comes nearer there is the view of the Warren - called 'Little Switzerland'. It is always a dream of beauty to lovers of Nature: the cliffs with their glory of gold, blue and white, the wealth of wild flowers, the deep ravines; the beach with its boulders flung about as if by giants in their sport; the growths of moss; sheltered nooks [where] lovers linger to explore; the trees rich in foliage and music; and the sea with its fantastic crests upon the waves and restless movement; all creating an impression upon memory that remains among the precious things of life.

On the other side of the Harbour there is the long stretch of the Leas. There England is green to the sea; the varied heights connected by winding paths between the trees, the resting-places of birds in song. The charm of the Lower Road with the toll-house and gate, and Sandgate Castle at the end, makes one of the prettiest picture postcards in the country. The steep cliffs and cable elevators remind one of Swiss scenery. Above, there is the table-land of the Leas, one of the finest promenades by the sea to be found in England, and one of the most popular health resorts in the world. On the Leas there is the strong tonic of the breeze; down on the Lower Road, sheltered from the winds, there is a warmer climate, so welcome to the invalid, and all round there is the panorama of beauty.

The Harbour is always a source of interest. Fishing boats come and go with their copper-coloured sails. The Market, with its quaint background of little cottages built into the cliff, tells a bit of history to any who care to learn. The Harbour is one of the main entrances to England, a favourite place for sea anglers, and those who find delight in watching the passing show of many-sided humanity never fail to discover a new phase.

The Leas presented an animated picture in July 1914. All varieties of fashion were represented along the famous promenade. The band - one of the best in the country – played at the end of the Leas, between the hotels Metropole and Grand. Behind, the hills stretched in their varied loveliness; Caesar's Camp and Sugar Loaf Hill stood out in all their glory of living green. The sky was as near the Mediterranean blue as one was likely to see in England. The ships going up and down the Channel provided endless interest and speculation; the sea was as calm as a mill-pond, and down the picturesque slope from the Leas to the beach the birds sang in the fir trees, and the children played among the bracken. Little did the happy throng of visitors dream that, just across the Channel, were all the preparations for a great war that would outrage Belgium and lay waste the fair fields of France; and that Britain within a few days would be plunged into a conflict such as the world had never known.

The retired captains played their golf in the morning, slept in the afternoon, managed to get a rubber of bridge in the evening, or occupied themselves with a discussion of the morning game and a pipe. The admirals, who had been on half-pay for more years than ladies cared to remember, strolled down to the seats by the shelter, and swept the sea with their glasses, discussed the character of the craft, then read their papers and dozed.

The band still discoursed on the Leas, but the gay crowd was not there. The boys were enlisting; they were exchanging the immaculate collars and cuffs for the soldier's garb. Women were asking what they could do, and were preparing for manifold kinds of service. The trade of the hotel proprietors and boarding-house keepers was at a standstill, and the outlook was very dark. The sunshine on the cliffs had still its glories of gold and blue. The Lower Road was as beautiful as before, and the birds sang just as sweetly; nature was all unconscious of the havoc man would make in the frenzy of war.

After the declaration of war on 4 August 1914, the grand hotels of the West End emptied as visitors fled this vulnerable corner of south-east England nearest the continent of Europe in fear of a German landing or naval bombardment from the sea. Within seven days of the declaration of war Folkestone was declared a prohibited area and all 'aliens' were required to register themselves and satisfy the authorities of their reasons to stay in the town. However, the numerous German and Austrian waiters who worked in the hotels and restaurants were rounded up and sent off to internment camps.

An early indication of the horror and misery to come was brought home to the people of Folkestone on 20 August 1914 when fishing boats and coal carriers crammed with frightened Belgian refugees and soldiers began arriving at the harbour with grim tales of rape, pillage and murder by their German neighbour. This proved to be excellent propaganda for the war effort and appeared to justify why Britain was at war. Carlile commented: 'The sight of those struggling companies of strangers going along the streets with their scanty belongings in bundles they would not trust to other hands presented a picture time will never

obliterate from the memory.' The Belgian Committee for Refugees was quickly constituted to provide food and shelter, which enabled 15,000 Belgians to settle in Folkestone and another 64,500 to pass through on their way to other parts of the country. Contingency plans were prepared in case Folkestone itself was invaded and an emergency committee was set up to prepare for the exodus of civilians and the destruction of foodstuffs and material likely to be of service to the enemy.

As in every other in city, town, village and hamlet in the kingdom, the young men of Folkestone and its neighbourhood eagerly answered the call to arms. They were drilled in Radnor Park and on the Leas before largely joining the local East Kent Regiment, known as the Buffs. The British Expeditionary Force in France had fallen back before the German steamroller and 100,000 volunteers had readily enlisted to bolster the small regular army. However, the situation looked bleak before the BEF rallied at the Battle of the Marne and pushed the Germans back for five consecutive days. The nation rejoiced and believed their boys would be in

German 'aliens' being marched through Sandgate on 10 August 1914. Marlinova Collection

Belgian refugees fleeing the mighty German army arrive at Folkestone Harbour in August 1914. Marlinova Collection

Berlin by Christmas, yet the Germans held their ground at the Battle of the Aisne and four years of mud and mindless slaughter lay ahead. For God, King and Country, 413 Folkestonians were to make the supreme sacrifice.

From February 1915 Canadian soldiers began to be based at Shorncliffe Camp on the outskirts of the town and within a year 40,000 of them were in training, housed in great camps on St Martin's Plain with shops, canteens, cinema and great rows of huts and tents. Over the next three years a further 100,000 of their countrymen came to the camp and it became a local joke that Folkestone and Hythe had been transformed into suburbs of Toronto! Locals began to adopt some of the Canadian expressions, such as 'sure' when meaning 'yes', and 'good eats' for a fine meal. To help prepare for what lay ahead, practice trenches were dug near Sandling Camp and at Seabrook. Folkestone itself became virtually a military garrison between 1916 and 1919 as four rest camps were set up in the town, to accommodate troops from all corners of the land on their way to the Western Front, or to reinvigorate those who had just returned from the action. By May 1919 nearly nine million men had passed through Folkestone on their way to the Front; proudly marching down the Slope Road (renamed the Road of Remembrance after the war) and onto the ships where many of them took their last ever look at the receding white cliffs of home (or their adopted home).

As the war progressed, Folkestone took on a shabby air as roads were churned into mud tracks by the heavy military traffic and shutters on abandoned and empty houses gave once-elegant streets a blank and lifeless aspect. From 1916 the Defence of the Realm Act (DORA) was strictly implemented, with Government control on food, pub opening hours, lighting and the press; and spies were said to be everywhere. DORA was described as becoming an obsession; 'a very real and terrible person with unlimited powers and a positive genius for butting in when she was least wanted'. Sugar, milk, margarine, butter and meat became especially hard to come by and coupons were eventually issued by the Government to combat profiteers letting food 'dribble' out so as to keep prices high. Eggs, for example, had jumped from 1d to 5d, bacon from 10d to 1s 8d and sugar 1 $^3/_4$ d to 5d. The only thing that seemed to be easily obtainable was marrow, and everyone soon became sick at the sight of it! For locals this food rationing caused increased hardship and municipal soup kitchens had to be set up in the poorer sections of the town in the East End and Fishmarket areas.

The shelling of Scarborough, Whitby and Hartlepool by German battle-cruisers early in the war, along with the subsequent raids by Zeppelins, had shown the home population the horrors of war were no longer confined to a far-away foreign field. However, for the first three years of the war Folkestone, despite being a front-line military town and so a legitimate target, had been spared enemy attention, though a raid on the nearby Otterpool Camp at Lympne on the night of 13/14 October 1915 had killed 15 Canadian soldiers. Nearby Dover, Ramsgate and Margate were targeted on a regular basis, so why not Folkestone? Many townsfolk believed they had been spared because local fisherman had rescued sailors from

During the war No. 3 Rest Camp for troops encompassed some of the houses and hotels in the select West End of Folkestone. Marlinova Collection

N°3 REST CAMP
EARLS AVENUE ENTRANCE
FOLKESTONE (N°12)

the sinking German iron-clad *Grosser Kurfürst* after a collision with its flagship *König Wilhelm* off the town on 31 May 1878. A large memorial to the 284 sailors who had perished had been placed in Cheriton Road Cemetery and the Germans were now repaying the favour by not attacking the town, despite its military importance as the main port for troop movements and its closeness to the large Shorncliffe Army Camp. Such was the belief in this sentiment that many townsfolk still could not believe an air raid was taking place on 25 May 1917 even while the bombs were raining down; and sadly this was to contribute to the high death-toll.

The German memorial in Cheriton Road Cemetery to the 284 of their sailors who lost their lives when the Grosser Kurfürst *sank in the Channel off Folkestone on 31 May 1878. Many townsfolk believed Folkestone would be spared German attention because of the help given to the sailors by local fishermen. Sadly, this was not to be the case and many of the innocent civilian victims of the raid lie in the same cemetery as the memorial.* Marlinova Collection

Chapter Two

THE WAR BROUGHT HOME

GERMAN ACTION OVER KENT, DECEMBER 1914 TO OCTOBER 1915

After the outbreak of war the Royal Flying Corps (RFC) sent their four squadrons to France with the BEF, leaving just a few elderly planes to man a woefully weak home defence. The Admiralty had formed their own Royal Naval Air Service (RNAS), which was largely deployed on anti-submarine duties. This lack of a unified command was to hamper an effective use of air defence and became a contributory factor in the success of some of the German air raids.

The initial threat came, however, not from German aircraft or airships, but the powerful battle-cruisers of the Imperial German Navy, each longer than a football pitch and home to around 1,400 men. The Naval Commander in Chief, *Admiral*

A patriotic postcard sold in Kent during the war. Note the white cliffs extending down to the Sussex border; in reality they end at Folkestone. Marlinova Collection

Friedrich von Ingenohl, was anxious to restore the spirits of his men after the loss of five ships at the Battle of the Falkland Islands on 8 December 1914 and sought to strike at the British mainland in a far more effective manner than the desultory shelling of Great Yarmouth on 3 November 1914, which had caused very little damage and no loss of life.

A plan was therefore devised to prise a British squadron away from the Grand Fleet and lead it to the guns of the German navy, while an advanced force of battle-cruisers led by *Admiral* Franz von Hipper shelled the east coast of England. The British soon caught wind of the plan, but were unsure when or where the Germans would strike. The area between the Tyne and the Humber had been declared a danger area due to the laying of a minefield by the Germans on 25/26 August 1914 and the British commander Admiral John Jellicoe decided to place his fleet some 25 miles south-east of the Dogger Bank, thinking that would be the best place to intercept the German fleet as they returned from a raid. On 15 December 1914 the German High Seas Fleet formed off Heligoland and set sail into the North Sea. A party of British destroyers was soon engaged and dealt with, yet von Ingenohl, thinking they were a part of a screen covering the British fleet, withdrew his ships leaving von Hipper's advance raiding party of five battle-cruisers and a light destroyer to steam on alone. In misty conditions they slipped through a gap in the minefield off Whitby and divided into two – the *Seydlitz*, *Moltke* and *Blücher* headed for Hartlepool, while the *Derfflinger*, *von der Tann* and the destroyer *Kolberg* set sail for Scarborough (the destroyer to lay mines off Flamborough Head).

The distinctive bird-like German Taube, often wrongly attributed by people in Kent with carrying out air raids on the county. Marlinova Collection

The Seydlitz, *one of the German battle-cruisers responsible for the bombardment of Hartlepool on 16 December 1914, in which 132 people were killed.* Marlinova Collection

As children got ready for school and sat down for breakfast, the bombardment of Scarborough commenced at 8.00 am on 16 December 1914, followed three minutes later by the first salvo on Hartlepool. This busy port had a small naval patrol and three 6-inch guns and therefore was classed as a legitimate target (if still largely defenceless). During the next 49 minutes it was hit by 1,150 shells that largely fell on residential areas, causing the death of 114 civilians (plus 18 military personnel), many of them dying as they ran panic-stricken through the streets. The shore battery did their best to harry the German ships and inflicted some minor damage, but they were hopelessly outgunned.

A postcard showing the damaged St Barnabas Church in Hart Road, Hartlepool after the naval bombardment of 16 December 1914. Marlinova Collection

The popular holiday town of Scarborough, on the other hand, was unprotected, though the Germans trained their guns first on that defensive relic of another age, the castle on the headland, which had a war-signal station and an old barracks that had not been used since 1878. However, as units of infantry and field artillery trained in the castle grounds, the Germans presumably thought the barracks were still in use. For 25 minutes 500 shells rained down on the town striking the imposing Grand Hotel, the Spa and the large hotels on the South Cliff, as well as residential areas. Eighteen people were killed, including a postman on his rounds, a 15-year-old Boy Scout on his way to collect a paper in which he was due to appear, and a 14-month old baby. A family living at 2 Wykeham Street lost four of its members when a shell destroyed the building, and amongst the many narrow escapes was a milkman whose horse and cart were blown away. The German cruisers could clearly be seen just a mile offshore and led many to assume an invasion was imminent, causing them to flee in panic with what few possessions they could carry. The *Scarborough Pictorial* commented:

> *People flocked from their homes in hundreds and distressing scenes were witnessed, no one knowing whether or not their houses would come toppling about their ears the next minute. Debris was falling in all directions. Innumerable windows were crashing in, and in many households where breakfast was in progress, crockery and furniture were massed in indescribable confusion. The roads were littered with bricks, tiles, slates and glass.*

At 8.25 am the battle-cruisers sailed north from Scarborough and 30 minutes later reached Whitby, an undefended fishing port. In 11 minutes 200 shells fell on the town and 4 people were killed. Among the buildings hit was St Hilda's Abbey, where the west arch was blown clean through. The two raiding parties then met up and slipped back through the minefield. In dense mist and rain-squalls they managed to avoid the British fleet and were able to safely reach port.

The reaction to the raid by the two belligerents was of course very different. The British were roused to great anger (some directed towards the inability of the Royal Navy to defend the towns) and recruitment soared to the cry of 'Remember Scarborough'. The Germans were understandably delighted at showing the British their island fortress was no longer impregnable, but for the neutral *New York Tribune* the raid had 'set a vicious and dangerous precedent in wantonly killing non-combatants, women and children among them, in undefended towns. Germany cannot escape responsibility for taking the first step from recognised practice in restoring barbarities which the world had hoped to eliminate from the practice of war.'

The German press claimed the first air attack against the British mainland was carried

Houses in Gray Street, Whitby damaged during the 16 December 1914 bombardment of the town by German battle-cruisers, in which four people were killed.
Marlinova Collection

The remains of a house in Wykeham Street, Scarborough where four members of the same family were killed during the German bombardment of 16 December 1914. Eighteen people were killed in the town.
Marlinova Collection

A Friedrichshafen FF29, from which the first bomb on British soil was dropped.
Archive Marine Luftschiffer Kameradschaft

out by a Taube of the German army unit *Feldfliegerabteilung 9*, with pilot *Leutnant* Karl Caspar and observer *Leutnant* Roos, which bombed Dover on 25 October 1914. However, there is no reference to this raid in British records. The first recognized attempted raid on Britain by an aeroplane occurred on 21 December 1914 when a Friedrichshafen FF29 piloted by *Leutnant* Stephan von Proudzynski of *Seefliegerabteilung 1*, based at Zeebrugge, dropped two bombs 400 yards south-west of the Admiralty Pier, Dover. Three days later von Proudzynski obtained the honour of dropping the first bomb on British soil, which landed harmlessly on a cabbage patch in the garden of Tommy Terson, near the rectory of St James's Church, Dover. The pilot, flying at around 5,000 feet, had to lift the bomb with both hands, control the joystick with his knees and then let it go. He was probably aiming for Dover Castle, but the net result was a crater of around 5 feet deep, some smashed windows in the rectory and bruises for Mr James Banks, who was knocked out of a holly tree he was cutting for Christmas decorations for the church. The AA Corps later presented fragments of the bomb to King George V, while on Boxing Day the Germans awarded the Iron Cross to von Proudzynski and also to *Fähnrich-zur-See* von Frankenberg, who had accompanied him as observer on the raid. On the following day, Christmas Day 1914, the pair returned to fly over North Kent and the Thames Estuary on reconnaissance before dropping two bombs just south of Cliffe railway station. The raider was chased by aircraft from Eastchurch, Joyce Green and Grain, yet made good his escape.

A fragment of the first bomb to drop on British soil in the First World War, at Dover on Christmas Eve 1914.
Marlinova Collection

Two Zeppelins carried out the first serious raid on Britain on the night of 19/20 January 1915, targeting Norfolk. Graf Ferdinand von Zeppelin had demonstrated the first rigid airship (LZ1) at Friedrichshafen on 2 July 1900. LZ1 was a progression from the earlier balloons with their single gas bag in that it contained multiple cells (of the highly explosive hydrogen) housed within a fabric envelope stretched around an aluminium frame. The multiple cells ensured that if any individual cell leaked there would still be enough gas to power the ship. In 1912 the Imperial German Navy took the lead in adapting the Zeppelins for use as bombers and were to become the main protagonists in the airship raids on Britain during the war. The German army, on the other hand, who also employed the plywood-based Schutte-Lanz (SL) airships, were to run their programme down as the war progressed, because of mounting losses. On 13 October 1912 it was reported a Zeppelin had passed over Sheerness and so began a spate of reported airship sightings around the country, all of which the Germans denied. However, the Imperial Naval programme got off to an inauspicious start when the first two airships were lost in 1913, but was then advanced with the appointment of the dynamic and convivial Peter Strasser, who inspired his men with confidence and pride. Each Zeppelin would normally carry a crew of between 18 and 25, housed in two gondolas situated underneath each end of the airship. The crew members had to be well insulated against the high altitudes they faced and were supplied with liquid oxygen to combat the thin air and altitude sickness. They were brave men who knew they had little chance of survival if the highly inflammable airship were to burst into flames.

In a bid to combat the Zeppelin threat, Allied planes had carried out raids against German bases between September and December 1914, but with only

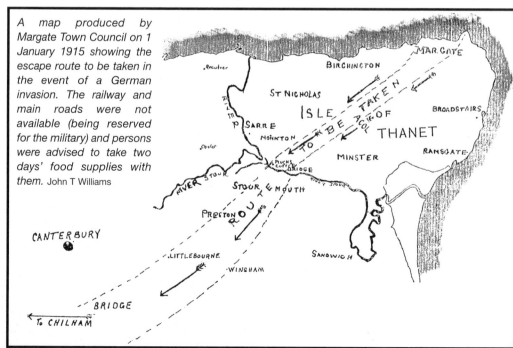

A map produced by Margate Town Council on 1 January 1915 showing the escape route to be taken in the event of a German invasion. The railway and main roads were not available (being reserved for the military) and persons were advised to take two days' food supplies with them. John T Williams

A wounded Mr Ellis stands outside the wreckage of his house in Lancaster Road, Great Yarmouth after the first Zeppelin raid on Britain during the night of 19/20 January 1915.
Marlinova Collection

limited success. The Kaiser had granted qualified approval for the aerial bombardment of Britain in January 1915 on the proviso that royal palaces and historic buildings were left alone and only coastal defences and industrial areas were to be targeted. Unfortunately, many industrial centres were located within large areas of population and even if the Kaiser did initially wish to avoid large civilian casualties, accurate bombing of this nature was just not technologically possible.

The Norfolk raid by Zeppelins L3 (builder's number LZ24) and L4 (LZ27) was to leave 4 dead and 15 injured. L3, commanded by *Kapitänleutnant* Hans Fritz, dropped 9 high-explosive (HE) bombs and 7 incendiaries on Great Yarmouth, killing Miss Martha Taylor (72) and bootmaker Samuel Smith (53), as well as destroying a number of properties. L4, under *Kapitänleutnant* Magnus Graf von Platen-Hallermund, flew over North Norfolk, bombing Sheringham and Snettisham, though the worst affected was Kings Lynn, where a Mrs Gazeley and 14-year-old Percy Goate met their end. Once again the Germans were very pleased with the outcome of the raid and the crews of the two Zeppelins were decorated with the Iron Cross.

I doubt if the pilot of the lone German army Albatros BII that raided Sittingbourne and Faversham on 16 April 1915 would have received the same accolade – for the only victim of the raid was a blackbird! The plane had crossed the Kent coast at around noon and

A souvenir postcard mocking the raid by a lone aircraft on 16 April 1915, of which the only victim was a blackbird! Marlinova Collection

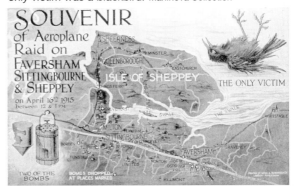

Wrecked House London Rd Southend-on-Sea

An inquisitive gathering stands outside the wrecked Cromwell Board Residence in London Road, Southend. The house was gutted by an incendiary during the Zeppelin raid of 10 May 1915. Marlinova Collection

The wrecked Bull and George Hotel in Ramsgate after a Zeppelin raid on 16/17 May 1915. Two guests were killed and the extensively damaged building had to be demolished. Marlinova Collection

after flying over Herne Bay and the Isle of Sheppey found itself over Sittingbourne, where it was fired upon by an anti-aircraft gun at Faversham. Circling the Gore Court Park (now King George's playing field) camp of the Royal Dublin Fusiliers, it dropped four HE bombs on Sittingbourne, but little damage was caused. Another bomb fell close to the Kingsferry Bridge, which linked the Kent mainland to Sheppey, before the raider made off to Faversham. Five bombs were aimed at the explosive works there, yet they all fell to the south, on the Mount cricket ground, Ashford Road, Mr Ratcliff's market-garden, an orchard at Mackinade Farm and hop gardens at Colkins. By this time a dozen machines had been scrambled from RNAS Eastchurch, Manston and Dover; however, the raider still escaped.

During a Zeppelin raid on Southend by LZ38 and LZ39 on 9/10 May 1915 a message was attached to a bomb, 'You English We Have Come and Will Come Again Soon – Kill or Cure, German'. Sure enough, it was Ramsgate's turn a week later, when LZ38, led by *Hauptmann* Erich Linnarz, dropped 4 HE and 16 incendiary bombs on the town in the early hours of 17 May 1915. One bomb struck the Bull and George Hotel in the High Street at 1.48 am (when the outside clock stopped); sending all the floors crashing down into the cellar, where John Smith was discovered,

An unusual postcard view of Mitchell's sweet shop, damaged by the Zeppelin raid of 16/17 May 1915 on Ramsgate.
Marlinova Collection

badly injured. He later died of his wounds, as did his wife, while barmaid Kate Moffat had a lucky escape when the bomb passed through her bed just after she had left it. The rest of the town escaped pretty lightly, though Mr France was injured when a bazaar on Albion Hill was wrecked, and another bomb glanced off the roof of the Star cinema in George Street and set fire to a fowl house in an adjoining garden. Also hit were Queen Street, Chapel Place, the grounds of St Catherine's Hospital, Ellington Park, St Lawrence, Nethercourt, Chapel Road (6 bombs) and Bell Cottages, rear of High Street (2 bombs). The premises of Mr Brackenbury, draper, of Queen Street were amongst those hit and he remembered:

> *About two minutes to two, we were awakened by the sound of exploding bombs which was followed shortly by the firing of rifles from the soldiers. As it happened, being Sunday night, there were only three shop assistants sleeping on the premises. We soon woke them up and took them down to the cellar. After the first explosion I got out of bed and looked out from the side of the window to see what was happening. I had not been there many minutes when a bomb which apparently fell at the back of the Bull & George, blew the whole of the bedroom windows out. Glass was blown all over the room, but luckily we escaped uninjured. Going to the room, which overlooks*

German army Zeppelin LZ38, responsible for the raid on Ramsgate on 16/17 May 1915. It was soon to meet its own end, however, when the airship sheds at Brussels-Evere were bombed on 7 June 1915. Marlinova Collection

Hauptmann *Erich Linnarz (the tall chap in the centre) and his crew of Zeppelin LZ38, which bombed Ramsgate on 16/17 May 1915.* Marlinova Collection

Queen Street, I saw the incendiary bomb fall opposite. It seemed to leap into a large flame, which spread up the road immediately it hit the ground. The windows in the cellar and the millinery and costume showrooms were also broken through concussion and earth was strewn all over the floor. At the back of the premises the damage was also severe. Small trees and stones were blown out of the adjoining garden and wedged tightly into the roof. Large quantities of earth were also thrown up to great heights. Pieces of the roof were torn away by the force of flying debris.

Flight Sub-Lieutenant Redford Mulock from Westgate Airfield in his Avro 504C had a go at the Zeppelin, but his gun jammed and it climbed out of reach. The airship then flew south and 33 incendiaries were dropped at Oxney, 3¹/₂ miles from Dover.

Linnarz certainly kept his Zeppelin busy and returned to Southend on 26/27 May 1915, when three people were killed. Five days later he carried out the first raid on London and seven people died, including four children. The inquest on Henry and Caroline Good of Balls Pond Road, Dalston left an impression on everyone who heard it. They had been found together burnt to death by an incendiary and Mr Good's arm was held around his wife's waist as they knelt by their bed in prayer. The death of little Elsie Leggatt, aged 3, buried beneath the ruins of 33 Cowper Road, Stoke Newington also shocked many people. Her brothers and sisters – May (11), George (10), Nellie (7) and Dorothy (5) – suffered serious burns and May later died of her injuries. Londoners responded by smashing up homes and businesses belonging to anyone with a German-sounding name. LZ38 was soon to meet its own end, however, when the airship sheds at Brussels-Evere were bombed.

In between the Southend and London raids Kent suffered its own tragedy when the minelayer *Princess Irene*, a newly converted passenger liner, exploded on 27 May 1915 while lying off Port Victoria, Isle of Grain. The dead numbered 278 officers and men, including 76 Sheerness Dockyard workers. There was only one survivor; a stoker named David Willis, who was discovered amongst the wreckage covered in thick black oil and barely alive. W G Moore in *Early Bird* recalled:

At Grain I saw the Princess Irene *blow up, possibly the most spectacular event I have ever witnessed. The* Princess Irene *was a C.P.R. Liner converted for mine laying. She was chock full of mines and was going out to sow them the next day. She was riding at anchor in Sheerness Harbour between our jetty and Port Victoria, only a few hundred yards out from the sea wall where I stood looking in her direction at the time. The whole thing was too awe-inspiring for me to appreciate the horror of it immediately. It started with stabs of flame spurting up from her deck from stem to stern, then a colossal roar, and everything was hurled into the air – a column of smoke then went up, up, up spreading out to a mushroom head at about 1,200 feet. Papers and light debris were picked up seven miles down-wind. The force of such an explosion seems to work in a parabolic curve and I was too close to get the full strength of the blast. I was blown on to my back but not stunned. The aeroplane hangar doors on the aerodrome behind me were all blown in and pieces of plate from the ship's side were found half a mile away in the marshes beyond the aerodrome. The oil storage tanks at Port Victoria were burst open and leaking as if they had been shelled. The Air Station launch, with its crew on board, was lying off our slipway so I hailed it and went with the Station Engineer Officer straight out to the scene of the disaster to see if we could pick up any survivors. We were the first launch there, but there was absolutely nothing to be found. There might never have been a ship there at all, save for the flotsam and oil. She had just disintegrated and sunk. As far as I know there were no survivors. Some of the crew were lucky. They were crossing the harbour in their liberty boat from shore leave in Sheerness when she blew up. There were rumours, of course, that the explosion was due to foul play – a time bomb, the work of a German spy. Others said the mines were being very carelessly primed by inexperienced ratings. Who is to know, she took her secret with her.*

Thousands of fragments of the ship and its contents, including the men aboard, littered the area for miles around. The Medway Towns were showered with pieces of furniture, naval caps, boiler suits, books and paper, even flesh, and a box of the ship's butter landed 6 miles inland from Rainham. A human head was found in a pond at Hartlip and another of a naval officer, complete with hat, was discovered at Grain. The body of a naval lieutenant was also found there with his gold rank stripes torn from his uniform and covering his face. Yet the saddest aspect of the disaster was the death of nine-year-old Ida Barden, who was killed by a piece of metal plate, which struck her in the head as she was playing in a garden at Grain. Labourer George Bradley (47) was also a casualty: he dropped dead in a field at Home Farm, Grain.

The minelayer Princess Irene *was the second vessel to explode in the Medway, on 27 May 1915. Of the 279 on board there was only one survivor, and among the dead were 76* Sheerness *Dockyard workers.*
Duncan Haws

The *Princess Irene* was the second vessel to have exploded in the Medway since the war began. Back on the morning of 26 November 1914 HMS *Bulwark* had blown up, killing 729 out of 741 on board and showering nearby areas such as Sheerness

HMS Bulwark, *which blew up in the River Medway on 26 November 1914 killing 729 of the 741 on board.* Marlinova Collection

and Rainham with debris. An eyewitness to the explosion, who was on board a ship nearby, remembered:

I was at breakfast when I heard the explosion, and I went on deck. My first impression was that the report was produced by the firing of a salute by one of the ships, but the noise was quite exceptional. When I got on deck I soon saw that something awful had happened. The water and sky were obscured by dense volumes of smoke. We were at once ordered to the scene of the disaster to render what assistance we could. At first we could see nothing, but when the smoke cleared a bit we were horrified to find the battleship Bulwark *had gone. She seemed to have vanished entirely from sight, but a little later we detected a portion of the huge vessel showing about four feet above the water. We kept a vigilant look-out for the unfortunate crew, but saw only two men.*

Sabotage was suspected, though the cause may possibly have been an accidental ignition of ammunition.

On the night of 4/5 June 1915 Sittingbourne and Gravesend were mistakenly targeted by L10 (LZ40) commanded by *Kapitänleutnant* Klaus Hirsch, who thought Gravesend was Harwich. Four HE and twenty-four incendiary bombs fell on Sittingbourne and Milton Regis, but little damage was caused save for the bomb that fell between Unity Street and Park Road, which damaged houses and injured two people. Bert Grant was six at the time and remembered:

My family had all gone to bed early because the raids were regularly taking place after dark. We got up when the siren sounded and all sat on the bed, listening to the sound of the Zeppelin going overhead. It passed over, so we knew we were safe, but then we heard a big bang quite close by and realised a bomb had been dropped. We all ran speedily downstairs, but because it was so dark we did not venture outside. Next morning, I remember my mother had already been to the bombsite by the time we'd got up. She said it was a miracle it had missed the church and a mercy no one had been killed – so I learned the difference between a miracle and mercy in one go.

Eight-year-old Nellie Webster was living with her grandparents in Unity Street:

The bomb dropped in the middle of the night and I remember we couldn't find any clothes because of the dark and confusion. We rushed out in our night clothes and someone picked me up to carry me down the road away from the damage.

The bomb had hit the back garden of a wall in Park Road and one woman had a lucky escape when a piece of shrapnel buried itself in the wall above her head. The three other bombs fell harmlessly on Jackson's Field, St Paul's Street and a wheat field at Chilton Farm.

The Zeppelin dropped one bomb at Twydall Farm, Rainham, killing a horse, before it arrived at Gravesend. Five HE and three incendiary bombs fell here and the damage was more extensive than at Sittingbourne. Houses were wrecked in Windmill Street, Wingfield Road, Peppercroft Street and two homes were demolished in Wrotham Road, burying the five occupants under rubble, though fortunately they were all pulled out alive. In Brandon Street an incendiary destroyed a stable, killing two horses, and a woman was struck in the face by shrapnel. Another bomb fell on a house in Cobham Street, but it was a dud, and others fell behind Woodville Terrace and Bath Street. The nurses' home at the general hospital was set ablaze, yet fortunately the majority of the nurses were on duty. However, a nurse suffered a dislocated shoulder when the VAD Military

On the morning after, a crowd has gathered to view the damage in Unity Street, Sittingbourne caused by the Zeppelin raid of 4/5 June 1915. Sittingbourne Library

Hospital based at the yacht club suffered serious blast damage. Six people in total (two men, three women and a child) were injured, though one solider in the yacht club had a fortunate escape:

> I had been operated on that afternoon and was coming round when I heard a rushing noise, and was just able to pull the sheet over my face. There was a shattering explosion, the window was blown out, and big pieces of plaster covered my bed and me. The iron cradle over my body saved my life, the doctor said.

L10 then floated off into the night, but was later destroyed in September 1915 when it was struck by lightning whilst venting oxygen.

Up to this point the raids by Zeppelins on Kentish towns had largely been ineffectual, yet elsewhere they had extracted a greater toll. Two days after the Sittingbourne raid, 24 people were killed during a raid on Hull, Grimsby and the East Riding of Yorkshire and on the night of 15/16 June 1915 Tyneside was badly hit with 17 people being killed at Palmer's engine works at Jarrow. Later in the year there were to be two particularly devastating attacks on 8/9 September 1915 (26 killed and 94 wounded in London, Norfolk and the North Riding of Yorkshire) and 13/14 October 1915 (71 killed and 128 wounded when five airships raided London, Norfolk, Suffolk and the Home Counties). Zeppelin L12 (*Oberleutnant* Werner Peterson) targeted Dover during the raid of 9/10 August (when Hull was hit again, with the death of 16 civilians) and one soldier later died in hospital when a bomb fell near the trawler *Equinox*. However, the airship was hit by the Langdon AA battery and came down in the sea. It was attacked by Dunkirk-based fighters whilst under tow and at Ostend fatally broke its back while being hauled onto the quay. This success followed on from the events of 6/7 June 1915 when Flight Sub-Lieutenant R A J Warneford destroyed LZ37 over Ghent and Flight Lieutenants Wilson and Mills bombed the airship sheds at Guère and obliterated Linnarz's LZ38. These losses seriously weakened the German army's airship campaign and their Army Airship Service was eventually abandoned in 1917.

The German navy, on the other hand, was acquiring more powerful Zeppelins, and in July 1915 permission was granted for the removal of all restrictions on the bombing of London (though the Kaiser insisted Westminster Abbey, Buckingham Palace and St Paul's should be left alone). On 17/18 August 1915 during a raid by three airships, one of them, L11 (LZ41) under the command of *Oberleutnant* Horst von Buttlar, flew inland over Herne Bay and was fired on by members of the 42nd Provisional Battalion. The ship passed over Whitstable and Canterbury before heading south to Ashford where 2 HE and 19 incendiary bombs were unloaded, causing little damage save to houses in Canterbury Road and Queens Road and to sheep and chickens near the sanatorium. The Zeppelin then flew towards Faversham, dropping 16 HE and 25 incendiary bombs in open countryside around Badlesmere on the way, with the damage limited to some broken windows in Badlesmere Church.

Regrettably, Zeppelins were not the only German menace on the home population of the county during 1915, for there were also occasional raids by small aircraft on coastal towns in East Kent. On 13 September 1915, just before dusk, bombs were dropped on Margate by a seaplane, sadly with fatal results. Four of the bombs fell harmlessly on the foreshore, but the other six landed amongst residential areas in the Cliftonville area of the town. Two women were seriously injured and later died; Agnes Robins (40), a lodging-house keeper at 26 Gordon Road, and Kate Bonny (27) of Brooklyn Lodge, Albion Road, who died in hospital four days after the raid. Kate had been standing at the gate of the house waiting for her parents to return when she was hit, and after her death she was laid to rest in Ramsgate's Jewish Cemetery. A further two men, three women and a child were injured. Two lady visitors enjoying tea in a room on the top floor of 14 Godwin Road were injured by the explosion of a bomb on the back of the building, and a nurse holding a child in her arms was wounded in the shoulder by a flying splinter while standing on the garden path of a house in Albion Road. A child of four was wounded, and Walter May and his fare had a fortunate escape when the two cab-horses were blown up in front of him in Albion Road. The raid was described at the time in a postcard sent by Kathleen Barratt to her grandmother in Warrington:

Just a card to let you know we are safe, you will hear of the air raid this evening. We are on the Green by the gap. Father had walked down by the chain and we were resting on the seat. We saw this thing pass exactly over our heads, very high, looked like an ordinary aeroplane, never dreamed it was an enemy one, it was not a Zepp. Then an awful bang, then another and another, till there were six at least – one fell in the gap, two on the sands, one in Queens Gardens, one in the Oval, one or more in Godwin Road. Great damage was done in Godwin Road to houses. Many broken windows at Malabar and houses below, and one house had the roof off. One soldier injured, perhaps more, saw the ambulance go in one house. A cat died of fright in Sweyn Road, I saw it lie down on the ground – of course father was upset, he jumped up and began to run away; I had to hold him by the waist to help him up. I soon brought him home and put him straight to bed, and he seems quiet now and says he is not nervous. I can hardly keep my wits together to write but I knew you would be anxious about us. We will send you a card again tomorrow to say how we are after the night – I wish it were morning now, love for mother.

The night of the Zeppelin raid of 13/14 October 1915, when 71 people were killed around the country, saw two of the five antagonists, L13 (LZ45) and L14 (LZ46), almost collide over Bickley. L13, led by the daring and most efficient of the Zeppelin commanders, *Kapitänleutnant* Heinrich Mathy, unloaded 3 HE and 14 incendiary bombs aimed for Woolwich Arsenal. Little damage was done, though a shop was burnt out in Thomas Street and nine men were injured, one of whom later died. L14 went to the other end of the county and at around 9.15 pm dropped four bombs on Otterpool Camp, Lympne. Fifteen men of 8 Howitzer Brigade and 5 Brigade of Canadian Field Infantry lost their lives and another twenty-one were injured: in addition seven horses were killed. After two HE bombs had been dropped on the racecourse at Westenhanger, *Kapitänleutnant* Alois Böcker directed the airship out to sea at Hythe, but having found his bearings then came inland again at Littlestone. The line of the coast was then followed as far as Pett, near Hastings, before L14 headed north. Seven incendiaries were dropped on Frant and three HEs on Tunbridge Wells, but little damage was caused. However at his next target, Croydon, nine people were killed by 18 bombs, including three brothers aged 15, 14 and 10.

The Zeppelins had had a good night, and though there were more to come in 1916, by the end of that year they were to be largely a spent force. East Kent, however, was to suffer its own particular problems over the coming year, with the ever more daring escapades of the German seaplanes.

Otterpool Camp, between Lympne and Sellindge, where 15 Canadian soldiers were killed during a Zeppelin raid on 13/14 October 1915. Marlinova Collection

Chapter Three

HIT AND RUN
IN EAST KENT

SEAPLANE RAIDS AND THE DEMISE OF THE ZEPPELINS, JANUARY 1916 TO APRIL 1917

The East Kent coast was just within the limited range of the German naval seaplanes based in Belgium and was subjected to a number of raids throughout 1916. The planes were often referred to at the time as a 'Taube' (meaning Dove in English), a familiar German aircraft with bird-like wings. However, this plane was usually used just for reconnaissance and the raids were carried out by a number of different seaplane types from various aircraft manufacturers, including Rumpler, Albatros, Friedrichshafen and Hansa-Brandenburg NW.

Dover was subjected to such a raid in the early hours of 22/23 January 1916 when eight HE bombs and one incendiary were dropped on the town by a Friedrichshafen FF33b, leaving one man dead and seven injured, including three children. The malthouse of the Phoenix Brewery was wrecked, as was the gas office in Russell Street and the Red Lion Inn in St James's Street when a bomb blew off its roof, killing barman Harry Sladen and injuring James Browning, George Gambrill and Richard Willis. Bombs dropped around Golden Cross Cottages injuring three children, including Daisy (14) and Grace (10) Marlow. Miss Julia Philpott (71) was injured whilst lying in bed. Houses in Waterloo Crescent, Cambridge Terrace, Camden Crescent and Victoria Park were also damaged in the raid. Twelve hours later, at noon, two seaplanes returned and unloaded five bombs on Capel Airship Station, but without much success. A further attack, on the 24th, was beaten off with no bombs dropped. After these attacks further anti-aircraft guns were placed at the castle, Fort Burgoyne, the eastern harbour arm and the Prince of Wales Pier.

Two planes, a Friedrichshafen FF33e and a Hansa-Brandenburg NW, raided Broadstairs and Ramsgate during the afternoon of 9 February 1916. Twelve bombs fell on Broadstairs, seven of them around the Bartram Gables girls' school. One pupil, nine-year-old Hermione Michaels, was injured, as was the housemaid Alice Earlop. The other five bombs fell at Tenerife, Dumpton Park Drive (where Miss Stevens was cut in the face by glass), the rear of Beresford House, Ramsgate Road and the garden of Beaumont House. Four bombs were aimed at Ramsgate, with one of them narrowly missing a crowded tramcar on the Broadstairs Road. The remainder fell harmlessly on open fields near Montefiore College.

Walmer was targeted on 20 February 1916 by a Friedrichshafen FF33, which

A Friedrichshafen FF33e, responsible for some of the 1916 seaplane raids on East Kent.
Marlinova Collection

aimed six bombs on the Royal Marine Barracks. Three of them fell harmlessly into the sea, but one hit the barracks, another landed in Dover Road, blowing out a great number of windows, and a third fell on Beach Road. Two boys standing talking by the iron railings of the barracks near the junction of Liverpool Road and the Strand were seriously injured and one, George Castle, later died. The other, Cyril Pedler, was first taken to the Royal Marine Infirmary on an old barrow and then to Deal Hospital in Wellington Road.

A lone FF29 took its chances against Thanet on 1 March 1916, but ended up crashing into the sea and was picked up by the French. However, it had managed to unload three HE bombs on Norfolk Road, Cliftonville, killing nine-month-old baby boy J W Dodman, and other bombs on Kingsgate and Broadstairs, causing some damage. The upper part of a house in Gladstone Road was wrecked and two bombs fell in Percy Avenue, smashing many windows. Another landed in the playground of an infants' school in Grosvenor Road and broke most of the windows in the building. Fortunately the children escaped unharmed, although a teacher, Miss Webb, received cuts to the face. King Edward Avenue and Victoria Gardens were also hit, and in Clarendon Road a bomb cut through a chain holding a dog to its kennel, allowing it to bolt to freedom!

The Zeppelins, meanwhile, were tending to leave this corner of England alone for now as they went for bigger fish to fry in London and the industrial heartlands of the Midlands and Yorkshire. On 31 January/1 February 1916 nine Zeppelins had raided Yorkshire, the Midlands and Suffolk, dropping a total of 205 HE and 174 incendiary bombs, which caused 70 fatalities and 113 wounded. Kent was briefly targeted, however, on 5/6 March during a raid by three airships on Hull (where 17 of the 18 casualties were killed), Lincoln and Leicester. After dropping bombs on the East Midlands, L13 (LZ45) drifted south and aimed four HE bombs on Sheerness. Fortunately they all fell wide of the mark, landing at Ripley Hill Marshes and Danley Farm, near Minster, with no effect.

On 19 March 1916, a concerted raid by six seaplanes (four Friedrichshafen FF33b, a Hansa-Brandenburg NW and a Gotha Ursinus WD) on Ramsgate and Dover left 14 dead and 26 wounded. On what was a very black day for the town, Ramsgate received 14 bombs from two of the planes, with devastating results. Five young children – Ernest Philpott (12), James Saxby (4), Gladys Saxby (8), Frank Hardwick and Herbert Gibbens – were killed in St Luke's Square as they made their way to Sunday school at St Luke's Church. Another little girl, nine-year-old Grace Ward, was found barely conscious clutching her bible. Her arm was found to be badly injured and later had to be amputated. Poor Grace never fully recovered from her injuries and died aged nineteen on 19 January 1926. Sixteen-year-old George Philpott, whose brother was killed, was another who never recovered from his injuries. He had become something of a hero after shielding his younger sister from injury, but in the process he suffered severe shrapnel wounds and the 'Human Shield', as he was dubbed, eventually died of his injuries early the next year. The bomb that killed the children had landed directly on the lap of driver H H Divers (49), and blew both him and his car to pieces. A sailor was unfortunate enough to witness the scene:

> There was a terrific explosion when the bomb dropped and the next thing I saw was the driver flung out of the car, which slid half a dozen yards before it came to a stop with a crash against the tree alongside me. I ran to three of the children who were lying in the roadway but I saw at once that the case of two of them was quite hopeless.

The other Ramsgate fatality was Mrs G M Bishop (23), who died two days later from shrapnel wounds. She had been married for just three months to a soldier on active service. Nine of the bombs fell around the gasworks, causing little damage, and others landed on the home of Mr T Desormeaux in Chatham Street, on Mr Blackburn's house-furnishing and undertakers in King Street, and Chatham House School, which was in use as a Canadian hospital. One Ramsgate resident vividly recalled the raid:

> Sunday, March 19th 1916 was a brilliant spring day and we were loitering over the dinner table when there was a sudden 'bang bang' and sounds of children screaming. We hurried out of doors and there in a main road, not more than fifty yards away, was a terrible sight. A bomb had fallen right on a passing motor car, hurling the driver yards away, dead, and killing outright a woman and five young children who were on their way to Sunday School. A young girl, Miss Kathleen Sykes, whom the bomb injured, lay for sixteen years a hapless invalid.

Margate was the recipient of just one bomb, which hit the HQ of the 9th Provisional Cyclist Company at 29-30 Fort Crescent. However, one of the raiders was set upon by Flight Commander Reginald Bone in his Nieuport 10, based at RNAS Westgate, who killed the observer before forcing the plane down into the minefields off the Goodwin Sands. The plane, an FF33, and surviving crew of *Flugmeister* Ponater and *Leutnant* Herrenknecht, was later towed to Zeebrugge.

Three other planes on 19 March raid headed for Dover, though nine bombs were also dropped ineffectively at Deal. *Dover and the War* takes up the story:

> On Sunday, March 19th, at 1.57 p.m. a big German seaplane, with dove-shaped wings, suddenly appeared over the Harbour at a height of some 5,000 feet. After dropping bombs in the Admiralty Harbour it dropped three bombs in Northfall Meadow. One of these fell on a hut occupied by men of the 5th Battalion of the Royal Fusiliers, and almost all the men in the hut were either killed or seriously injured, four being killed or afterwards dying from injuries, and eleven injured. The guns by this time opened fire, but the aeroplane continued to fly directly over the town, dropping a bomb into the building ground in Castle Place directly behind Mr

Webber's shop, 12 Castle Street, and other bombs fell behind 50 Castle Street and in the cooper's yard of Messrs Leney and Co. The next bomb to fall was in Folkestone Road. It hit the tram track and blew in the fronts of the shops opposite St John's Terrace. Miss Edith Stokes, a domestic servant in the employ of Mrs P Hart, of Maison Dieu Road, whose parents lived at 18 Church Road, was cycling to Folkestone and was driven by the force of the explosion into the doorway of Mr Tarrant's shop, No. 131 Folkestone Road. She was dreadfully injured, and died later at the Dover Hospital. A little boy, Francis Hall, aged seven years, of 23 Winchelsea Street, who was on his way to Sunday school, hearing the gunfire, ran back towards home, and his mother, who had come to meet him, saw him killed by this bomb. The seaplane released two more bombs in this neighbourhood, one of which struck 152 Folkestone Road, doing a great deal of damage, and another fell at the rear of 107 Folkestone Road, facing the Ordnance Stores. The bomb just missed the roof gutter, and burst in the back yard, blowing out the back room. Neither of these bombs caused any casualties. The aeroplane then flew over the Western Heights, dropping two bombs on the grass bank just above Christ Church Schools. The next bomb fell in the back of the workshop of Mr Barwick, in Northampton Street. This one killed Mrs Jane James, a restaurant proprietress of 40 Snargate Street, and very seriously wounded Mrs Maude Lloyd, so that she had to have her right arm amputated, and the left was seriously hurt, and slightly wounding Mrs Florence Collier. Another bomb dropped in the Wellington Dock near to a gunboat, and two more fell into the Commercial Harbour. Whilst this attack was in progress another hostile seaplane of exactly the same type appeared over the Castle, whilst at the same time a small scout machine was seen going up at great speed from the Swingate Aerodrome to attack the first raider. When well over the town and apparently about to engage the raider, the engines of the British machine failed, and the machine had to come down, making a safe landing in the field on top of the hill just beyond the Citadel Battery. The second raider, after dropping some bombs on the Castle, dropped another on the Convent in Eastbrook Place. The convent was crowded with inmates, but, fortunately, the bomb exploded on the roof, and only one of the sisters, Sister Vincent, was injured by glass shattered by the explosion. This raider circled round the centre of the town, dropping a bomb on Mr Hogben's straw store in Church Street, which blew in the roof, one (which did not explode) through the roof of Mr Carder's office in King Street, another struck a bottle store of Messrs Leney and Co.'s mineral water manufactory in Russell Street, completely wrecking the building, another fell in the garden of Castle Hill House, whilst another bomb burst in the trees that grow in the garden at the corner of Woolcomber Street and Trevanion Street. The base of the bomb drove deeply through the asphalt pavement, and pieces of it penetrated the roof of Old St James's Church, and did a good deal of damage. The next two bombs fell at East Cliff, one in the front garden of an empty house, and the other in the roof of Mr Watson's house, East Cliff, blowing in the roof, whilst three more bombs fell into the sea in front of the waterplane sheds. The raid lasted some fifteen to twenty minutes and seven were killed and about thirty injured.

Yet, as at Ramsgate, one of the raiders was downed, this time by Flight Lieutenant R Collis in the Strait of Dover.

One of the mighty Zeppelins themselves was brought down 15 miles off Margate on 31 March/1 April 1916 on a raid by five airships during which 48

The end of Zeppelin L15 after it was hit by anti-aircraft fire: it is seen here sinking in the Thames Estuary on Saturday, 1 April 1916. Marlinova Collection

people were killed. L15, under the command of *Kapitänleutnant* Joachim Breithaupt, had crossed the Suffolk coast at 7.45 pm, but later came under heavy gunfire from the Purfleet-Erith-Plumstead area and at 9.45 pm it received a direct hit from the Purfleet gun. Second Lieutenant Albert de Bathe Brandon in his BE2c caused further damage, before the airship became nose-heavy and the crew jettisoned anything movable in a bid to reach Belgium. However, the ship broke its back and had to ditch in the sea just after 11.00 pm. All of its crew, bar Albrecht, who was drowned, were picked up by the armed trawler *Olivine* and transferred to HMS *Vulture*, which took them into custody at Chatham Dockyard. When questioned about his feelings on the killing of women and children Breithaupt replied: 'You must not suppose that we set out to kill women and children, we have higher military aims. You would not find one officer in the German Army or Navy who would go to kill women and children. Such things happen accidentally in war.' Efforts were made to tow the airship into port, but it foundered off Westgate and sank. The remains, including the body of poor Albrecht, were brought up onto Margate Sands for inspection and then were allowed to disappear under the shifting sands.

On 2 April 1916 the people of Faversham were enjoying their Sunday lunch when at 1.20 pm they were rocked by a huge explosion. The town was an important centre for the production of TNT, dynamite and other explosives based at two sites, the Cotton Powder Company (founded 1873) and the Explosives Loading Company (1912), on the Uplees Marshes. At around 12.10 pm sparks from a boiler house on the Explosives Loading Company's site had set fire to empty linen sacks piled against building No. 833 used to store TNT and ammonium nitrate. The fire burned slowly for 70 minutes before 150 tons of ammonium nitrate and 15 tons of TNT blew up with such force it could be heard as far away as Norwich. The ELC's four-man manual pump was assisted by the CPC's fire brigade in trying to fight the blaze and a bucket chain was formed involving 200 men. However, two further explosions at 1.40 pm and 2.00 pm set virtually the whole complex ablaze. George Goldfinch was running alongside a dyke towards a blazing shed when an explosion occurred and the next thing he remembered was finding himself on the other side of the water with all his clothes blown off. Yet he was one of the lucky ones, as recorded by Dr Charles Evers, who attended the scene and noted the vagaries of the explosions: 'Two men were side by side – one was killed instantly, the other hardly hurt. A number of men 30-40 yards away were unharmed, while men 100 yards away were blown to pieces. Men had all their clothes blown off them and yet were unhurt.' The total number of people killed (all men) has been put at between 106 and 116, though the memorial in Faversham Cemetery records 73 people were interred in the mass grave there, while 35 were buried elsewhere. This would put the final total at 108.

The German battle-cruisers *Derfflinger*, *Moltke* and *von der Tann* returned to bombard the east coast once more on 25 April 1916, with Lowestoft this time the target selected as part of a joint operation with six Zeppelins on eastern England. The bombardment began at 4 am and lasted for half an hour, during which 240 properties were damaged and four people were killed. Three of the deceased,

The mass grave in Faversham Cemetery, pictured on 6 April 1916, where 73 of the estimated 108 people killed in the gunpowder explosion of 2 April 1916 were laid to rest. Marlinova Collection

The remains of North End after the bombardment of Lowestoft by German battle-cruisers on 25 April 1916. Marlinova Collection

Sydney Davey, his sister Annie and nine-month-old Robert Mumfield, were killed when 20 Sandringham Road was hit, while at North End a shell pinned lodger W Hollins of Westcliff-on-Sea under a heap of rubble and he died after the house burst into flames. Another shell travelled through 13 houses in Kent Road, but failed to explode, and amongst the other areas damaged were the Esplanade, Cleveland Road, Yarmouth Road, Ashby Road, Kirkley Run, Stephen Street, Windsor Road, Carlton Road and London Road South. The arrival of the Harwich Flotilla led the German ships to abort the shelling.

A day later, during a raid by four army airships, Zeppelin LZ87 (*Oberleutnant* Barth) visited the Kent coast at around 9.55 pm. The airship aimed eight HE bombs at the steamer *Argus*, moored at Deal, before being driven off by guns at Walmer. LZ88 (*Hauptmann* Falck) passed over Herne Bay, Whitstable (one bomb landed on John Carr's baker's shop in Oxford Street), Sturry, Canterbury, Bridge, Wingham, Preston (nine HEs dropped), Sarre and Chislet Marshes (thirteen incendiaries) and St Nicholas-at-Wade, where a bomb landed in the vicarage garden, uprooting two trees, which fell against the house. An incendiary bomb landed on the sea wall at Minnis Bay, Birchington and three HE bombs fell in the bay itself.

Army Zeppelin LZ93 (*Hauptmann* Wilhelm Schramm) dropped three bombs off Deal during the night of 26/27 April 1916, and on 3 May 1916 the town was targeted again, this time by a Hansa-Brandenburg NW seaplane. Nine bombs fell on the town at about 3.30 pm, six of them around the railway station. One fell on an outhouse near the station, severely injuring a ticket collector, and another fell close by in the road maiming a house invalid. One of the bombs wrecked the

Admiral Keppel pub in Upper Deal when it fell right through the building without exploding, and a house in Albert Road was also badly damaged. A young milkman was among the injured and his son Charles Hutchins recalled:

The boy doing the milk round was actually my dad, Charles Henry Noel Hutchins, and he was hit in the leg by shrapnel from the German bomb. At the time he was in the area near Sutherland Road and went to quieten the pony pulling his milk chariot after a bomb had exploded near Deal railway station, injuring Mr Potnell, a railway station staff member. He and my father ended up in the old Deal Hospital in Wellington Road, where sadly Mr Potnell lost his leg. My Dad nearly lost his too, and my Mother still has the piece of shrapnel the surgeon extracted. The pony by the way was unscathed.

Seven planes took part in a raid on the East Kent coast during the night of 19/20 May 1916. The first raider unloaded fifteen bombs in the Victoria Avenue area of St Peters, Broadstairs, before dropping a further seven near the Whitfield Monument, the Electric Tramway Depot, Rumsfield's Waterworks, a farm at Bromstone and Pear Tree Cottage, Dumpton, where a chicken was killed. Another of the planes came into Kent over Sandwich and dropped nine bombs near the Small Downs Coastguard Station and three on Ramsgate. Further south, three planes targeted the area around Deal and Dover. Nine bombs fell on Sholden, one just missing the Chequers Inn, and ten on open fields at Ringwould. Dover was the recipient of fifteen bombs; one of them seriously damaging the Ordnance Inn in Snargate Street. Private H Sole of the 3rd Battalion, East Surrey Regiment, was killed when a bomb fell close to the Shaft Barracks. Mrs Bridges Broxham was injured by a bomb that fell on Military Hill, and another that landed on the Commercial Quay wounded deckhand James Harvey of HM Drifter EES. A number of the bombs fell around Dover College, greatly alarming the boys, but causing little damage. Flight Sub-Lieutenant R S Dallas in his Nieuport Scout brought down one of the raiders, and another was reported lost. Dover was further attacked on 9/10 July 1916, when seven HE bombs from a Friedrichshafen FF33h landed in the vicinity of Castlemount Cottages (causing little damage), and on 12 August 1916 when a Roland Scout seaplane, piloted by a frequent visitor to this coast, *Leutnant* Walter Ilges, dropped four bombs amidst intense AA fire. One fell in the harbour and another caused slight injuries to seven soldiers on parade at Fort Burgoyne. Seven RNAS planes gave chase, but Ilges escaped once again.

On the night of 24/25 August 1916, Zeppelins L31 (LZ72) and L32 (LZ74) paid a visit. L31 came in via Margate and unloaded 35 HE and 8 incendiary bombs on Deptford, Greenwich and Blackheath, killing eight. L32, meanwhile, was engaged on a curious zigzag course between the English and French coasts. The ship flew over Thanet, Dover and Folkestone, but was driven off by AA fire and the HE bombs released fell harmlessly into the sea.

The night of 2/3 September 1916 was to mark a turning point in the war against the Zeppelins when home morale was boosted to great effect by the shooting down of army airship SL11 at Cuffley by 19-year-old Lieutenant William Leefe Robinson of 39 Squadron. Robinson became an instant national hero and three days later was awarded the VC. The burning airship could be viewed from the North London suburbs and people flocked out into the streets to celebrate the death of *Hauptmann* Wilhelm Schramm and his 15 crew. Up to 60,000 curious souls descended on the

Hertfordshire countryside to view the remains of the dreaded 'Baby Killer' and for a moment the food shortages, the heavy losses of their loved ones on the Western Front and the air raids themselves were forgotten.

Three weeks later, on the night of 23/24 September 1916, during a raid by twelve airships, two of the new 'Super Zeppelins' were brought down. L33 (LZ76), commanded by *Kapitänleutnant* Alois Böcker, was hit by a shell and then suffered further damage to the fuel tanks from Albert de Bathe Brandon, in his BE2c, who had assisted in the earlier destruction of L15. The Zep gently came down in a field at Little Wigborough, near Mersea Island, Essex and none of the crew was badly hurt. An attempt to destroy the airship failed and the frame survived virtually intact; indeed it was later used to model the post-war British airships R33 and R34.

The other casualty was L32 (LZ74), led by *Oberleutnant* Werner Peterson. Having been caught in the searchlights over London, it was attacked by Second Lieutenant Frederick Sowrey in his BE2c and crashed in flames at Snail's Hill Farm, Great Burstead, Essex with the loss of all of its 22 crew.

During the same raid, Heinrich Mathy had aimed 1,280lb of bombs at Dungeness Lighthouse to lighten his load before causing death and destruction in London. However, just a week later, on 1 October 1916, he too was to perish when his L31 (LZ72) was shot down at Potters Bar by Second Lieutenant Wulstan Tempest. The brave and redoubtable Mathy was hero-worshipped in Germany (the British, of course, described him as an arrogant murderer) and his loss was a serious body-blow to the Naval Airship Division from which they never fully

All that was left of Zeppelin L32, which crashed in flames at Snail's Hill Farm, Great Burstead, Essex on 23/24 September 1916 with the loss of all of its 22 crew members.
Marlinova Collection

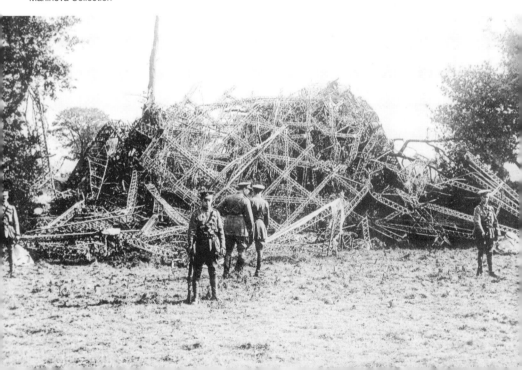

Three celebrated Zeppelin killers. On the left is Lieutenant William Leefe Robinson VC, who shot down the first Zeppelin (SL11) over Britain at Cuffley on 2/3 September 1916. He later became a prisoner of war and died of influenza on 31 December 1918. In the centre stands Second Lieutenant Wulstan J Tempest DSO who downed Zeppelin L31 at Potters Bar on 1 October 1916. On the right is Second Lieutenant Frederick Sowrey DSO, who shot down Zeppelin L32 at Great Burstead, Essex on 24 September 1916.
Marlinova Collection

recovered.

Two further airships, L21 (LZ61) and L34 (LZ78), were lost on 27 November 1916 and the campaign was halted in the face of a tightened home defence that had been reinforced with a ring of guns around London, observer posts and phone control centres. However, it had been the formation of Home Defence squadrons equipped with Buckingham tracer incendiary bullets and Brock and Pomeroy explosive/incendiary bullets that had been largely responsible for bringing the raiders down in the past two months. The Zeppelins would rarely venture back in such strength again, yet they had been partially successful in their task of weakening home morale (though the call for revenge was louder than the call for peace) and disrupting industry (it was said one-sixth of normal munitions production was lost). Furthermore, up to twelve flying squadrons were retained at home to deal with the raids, so weakening air power at the front line.

The sporadic nature of enemy action during the winter of 1916/17 led to the assumption that the Zeppelins, and perhaps German air raids in general, were largely a spent force. Complacency crept in and the home defences were weakened as planes were transferred to the Western Front. Four RFC squadrons remained to defend London and Kent (though the coastal strip between Dover and New

Romney was to be left disastrously undefended), yet they were made up of obsolete aircraft that could fly only at modest altitudes. In addition, the ground-to-air signalling available for the pilots was rendered ineffective because of the lack of proper training on the system, and anyway it took too long to lay out the Ingram Code of dots and strokes. In March 1917 defences were further weakened when an order was passed forbidding inland (but not coastal) AA guns to fire on enemy aircraft because of manpower having been transferred to France. The country's AA defence system was effectively silenced, despite reports circulating that a build-up of a new type of enemy bombing aircraft, the Gotha, was underway in the Ghent area.

Yet for East Kent the enemy threat was as real as ever. On 23 October 1916 two people were injured in Margate when a bomb from a seaplane fell on the roof of the St George's Hotel, Lewis Avenue. A day earlier Sheerness had also been targeted with four bombs. On 25 February 1917 it was the turn of the Kent coast to be bombarded from the sea when destroyers shelled the area around Margate and Broadstairs for ten minutes. One shell struck a cottage at Reading Street near Broadstairs occupied by Mr and Mrs Morgan and their six children. Mrs Morgan was killed instantly and her baby daughter Phyllis, clasped to her breast, died soon afterwards. Nine-year-old Doris later died in hospital and two of the other children were injured. Forty shells fell on Margate (damaging property in Eastern Esplanade, Norfolk Road, Empire Terrace and Ramsgate Road), Garlinge and Reading Street: some had been aimed at the North Foreland Lighthouse, but missed. Three weeks later, on 18 March 1917, Ramsgate underwent a three-minute bombardment from the sea. The four German destroyers had sunk HMS *Paragon* in the English Channel and seriously damaged the destroyer HMS *Llewellyn*. The SS *Greypoint*, a collier anchored off Ramsgate's East Cliff, was attacked and sunk, as was the small armed drifter *Redwald*, four of the crew being injured. In the town itself, houses were struck in St Ann's Road, including No. 34. However, the occupant, a Mrs Standen was forewarned by a premonition that her house would be hit and had moved in with a neighbour.

Four of the most able Zeppelin commanders: **top:** *left; Heinrich Mathy (killed 1 October 1916),* **right**; *Alois Böcker (killed 24 September 1916), bottom: left; Joachim Breithaupt (captured 1 April 1916)* **right**; *Peter Strasser (head of the German Naval Airship Division – killed 6 August 1918).* Marlinova Collection

The Zeppelins returned to Kent on the night of 16/17 March 1917, when five passed over the county and neighbouring Sussex. Four HE bombs were dropped on Swingfield, four incendiaries on Hougham, two HE and seven incendiary bombs on Newchurch, three HE and seven incendiaries on Appledore and one HE at Ivychurch, which killed four sheep. One of the raiders, L39 (LZ86), was later destroyed by French gunfire at Compiegne: this was the same airship that had dropped the largest bomb to fall in the Dover area, a 600lb that landed harmlessly on Windless Down in a corner of Long Wood. Two seaplanes also raided Thanet on the 16th, dropping thirteen bombs on Westgate and seven on Garlinge. The only real damage caused was to houses in Belmont Road and the seafront bandstand at Westgate.

On 21 April 1917 a squadron of six German destroyers became badly unstuck when bombarding Dover. All but one of the shells fell outside the borough with no effect whatsoever, and then as they withdrew, Commander Evans of the Dover Patrol gave chase with the destroyers HMS *Broke* and HMS *Swift*. Two of the German ships, G42 and 685, were sunk and three more were seriously damaged, leaving 28 German sailors dead, and 140 were captured. The British lost 24 men. Yet despite their losses, the Germans were not deterred and on the night of 27 April 1917 carried out the 'Hurricane Bombardment' on Ramsgate, Manston and Margate, when 300 shells were fired in only two minutes. In Ramsgate 22-year-old Ivy Thorncroft was fatally injured at 1 Upper Dumpton Park and her sister Hilda suffered severe injuries (a 2-inch piece of shrapnel was taken out of her leg two years later). The other direct fatality was 61-year-old John Hobday, at 32 Alma Road, and nearby John Belsey (57) was seriously wounded from shrapnel, as was Jessie Giles. Two elderly residents – Mrs Florence Cassidy (60) of 20 St Mildred's Road and James Barnes (73) of Clovelly, 21 Southwood Road – both died of shock. The St Luke's area of Ramsgate was once again badly hit, with the public bar of the Alexandra Arms in St Luke's Avenue being wrecked and damage occurring in Belmont Road, St Ann's Road, Boundary Road and Southwood Road. RNAS Manston received 37 shells; one of them damaging Ferndale in the village, the home of E E Philpott, and another 180 fell on the Thanet hinterland at Lydden Fleet, St Peters, Northwood, Dumpton, Westwood and Upton. The final eight shells fell on Margate, where a woman and her children were injured at 21 Addiscombe Road, and damage occurred in Vicarage Lawn, St Peters Road and Nash Road.

Notwithstanding the frequency of attacks on East Kent coastal towns, civilian casualties had so far been relatively light. However, for one town, as yet untouched by any enemy action, things were going to take a serious turn for the worse: the Gothas were gathering in Belgium.

Chapter Four

THE BIRTH OF
THE SILVER BIRDS

A NEW THREAT:
THE GERMAN GOTHA BOMBERS

The German army bombing unit *Fliegerkorps der OHL* was formed in 1914 after the demand by German *Grossadmiral* Alfred von Tirpitz for massive air attacks against London. In the words of the German historian *Major Freiherr* von Bülow:

> *The main purpose of the bombing attacks was the intimidation of the morale of the English people, the crippling of their will to fight and the preparation of a basis for peace. The secondary purpose of the raids was to disrupt the British war industry, disorganise the communication between the coastal ports and London; attack supply dumps of coastal ports and hinder transport of war materials across the Channel. The target of the raids was confined principally to London because it was the heart of England, the operational headquarters of the Allies and the centre of its war industry.*

However, plans to bomb Britain by aircraft from the Pas de Calais so as to be in range were thwarted when the German Fourth Army was held by the British at Ypres. For the time being, therefore, they had to be largely limited to towns and defences behind enemy lines, although, as we have seen, hit-and-run raids were carried out on the East Kent coast by naval aircraft.

Two years into the war, the German High Command drew up a strategy to reduce the pressure on its hard-pressed land forces, exhausted by the titanic struggle on the Somme, based on two specific countermeasures. They were unrestricted submarine warfare against Allied shipping, which though successful in greatly increasing British shipping losses brought the United States into the war, and the bombing of London by long-range aircraft, first envisaged in 1914 but now made possible by the strides made in producing suitable bomber aircraft.

Specifications for the production of a large bomber were given to several aircraft companies including Gothaer Waggonfabrik AG and in 1916 their Gotha GI, a German army design, went into production followed soon after by the first true Gotha designs, the GII and GIII. However, these two prototypes proved unsatisfactory, mainly because of engine problems, and were soon withdrawn from service. The requirements needed for a long-range bomber to be able to attack London and return home safely were finally met with the production of the Gotha GIV, which began in September 1916. In November 1916 the German army established an air force under a separate branch called the *Kogenluft* and in early

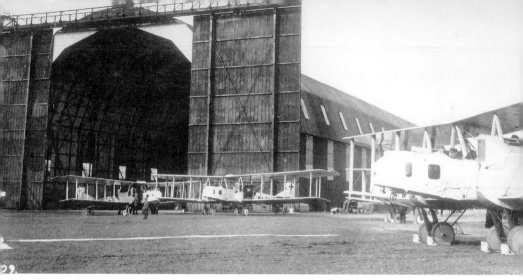

Gothas in front of the big Zeppelin hanger at Melle Gontrode. Thomas Genth

1917 *Kampfgeschwader der Obersten Heersleitung* 3 (KG3), otherwise known as KAGOHL III or *Englandgeschwader* (England Squadron), was formed under the command of 34-year-old *Hauptmann* Ernst Brandenburg. In December 1917 it was to be renamed *Bombengeschwader der Obersten Heersleitung*, or BOGOHL III. The operation was to be known as Turkencreuz (Turk's Cross) and was classified as top secret to ensure the element of surprise. It was envisaged that every assault would consist of at least 18 planes, each carrying 300kg of bombs, with London the main target, though in the event of bad weather, military sites, lines of communication and coastal towns would be hit. The main aim of the attacks remained the same; to force withdrawal of forces from the Western Front to bolster UK defences and create such panic amongst the population that some sort of peace settlement favourable to the Germans would be brought about.

Four airfields were laid out for the GIV in Belgium around Ghent (40 miles behind the lines) at Melle-Gontrode, St Denis-Westrem, Mariakerke and Oostacker. However, the first two were not ready until April 1917 and the others July so the few Gothas equipped by March had to be stationed at Ghistelles, only 10 miles behind the lines. The production target of 30 planes by February 1917 had proved to be totally unrealistic as the factories struggled with production and supply difficulties. The first test flights showed that the aeroplanes were far from operational and a lot of work and modification was necessary before the first sortie against England could take place. The morale of the crews was to be strongly tested by the delay, as they were keen to get involved in the fighting and, furthermore, from all parts of the Front there was a call for more planes and pilots. Yet they remained loyal to KAGOHL III and assisted in preparing these sick birds for a mission they were unsure would ever come.

Each Gotha was to have a crew of three: pilot, rear gunner and the commander, who was also the navigator, bomb releaser and front gunner. Commanders were normally officers from the time before the war who also had some experience in fighting with infantry. The skill of the pilot was essential, especially after a six-hour flight when the plane was empty and low on fuel (70 per cent of all Gotha losses were due to landing accidents). They were normally recruited from soldiers of all military ranks who, aside from their keenness had shown exceptional talent in flying these awkward aircraft. Last, but certainly not least, was the rear gunner with his two machine guns, whose hour came when an enemy fighter attacked the Gotha from the rear. Though they were mainly of a lower rank, usually a *Vizefeldwebel*, their task was not to be underestimated and many Gothas survived because of the bravery of these men. The Gotha crews were not born monsters, enjoying the killing of innocent civilians, but were professional soldiers; patriots, believing in the same traditions as their counterparts in every other civilized nation.

Adolf Genth was one of those soldiers; he shared with his comrades the same military education, being sent at the age of 11 to the *Kadettenanstalt*, where his civilian life was ended long before it had a chance to start. Adolf was born in the Transvaal, South Africa on 27 July 1894; the third son of Georg Genth, who had left Germany in 1890 to manage a forestry plantation for a British company producing quick-growing trees for timber. It is therefore possible that Adolf may have held British nationality for a time, though there is no firm evidence of this. The British

Hindenburg's *visit to KAGOHL III in Spring 1917.* Thomas Genth

victory in the Boer War in 1902 led to the Genth family returning to Germany, Georg, like most of his countrymen having favoured the Boer side because of his homeland's intense political rivalry with Britain.

Back in Germany Adolf's parents decided he should pursue a career as a soldier and to obtain a good military education he was sent to the *Kadettenkorps* Oranienstein in 1905 and then in 1910 to the *Hauptkadettenanstalt* at Gross-Lichterfelde. He became *Leutnant* of 4. Magdeburg Infantry Regiment NR67 in 1914 and fought with them in the early stages of the war at Argonne. After being severely wounded on three occasions – his left arm becoming weakened due to a bullet wound – he joined the *Kaiserliche Fliegertruppe* and started a new career as an aerial observer in July 1916. His training for this task took only three months, during which he learned to take aerial photos and defend himself whilst in the aircraft. On 10 October 1916 he joined *Kampfgeschwader* 1 and flew for the first time over the Western Front on the Somme before later in that year switching to KAGOHL III.

Adolf's new plane, the Gotha, was a giant with a span of 77 feet and a length of 41 feet making it easily the largest aircraft in the German forces up to that point. It was powered by two 260hp six-cylinder water-cooled Mercedes engines and had a roomy

The Genth family with guests in front of the farm in South Africa c. 1900. Adolf is second from left in the child's row. Thomas Genth

A young Adolf Genth, on the left, pictured shortly after the family's arrival back in Germany. With his elder sister's arm around him, Adolf appears to be holding a cricket bat, perhaps a souvenir from South Africa. Thomas Genth

Gotha GIV 406/16, the plane of Adolf Genth, pictured shortly before a test flight in Spring 1917. Thomas Genth

cockpit for the three crew. The weaponry consisted of three 7.92mm Parabellum machine guns: one at the front and two at the tail end for the rear gunner, who could fire either above the fuselage or through an open tunnel under the tail of the bomber using armour-piercing Mauser bullets with a tracer bullet every fourth round for accuracy. The Goerz bombsight enabled potentially greater accuracy with the bombing. Each plane was able to carry up to 300kg of TNT/hexanitrodiphenylamine 12½kg or 50kg anti-personnel bombs. The 50kg was the more potent weapon and could destroy a three-storey house with a direct hit, yet its fuses, designed to explode on impact, were notoriously unreliable and nearly a third of all these bombs dropped proved to be duds or they exploded prematurely, thereby weakening the overall potential of each raid. The 12½kg proved to be the more reliable, with a detonation success rate of 90 per cent. Two of the bombs were carried under the nose to compensate for the tail-heaviness of the GIV; but after their release this design flaw caused problems for the planes when trying to land and there were numerous crashes. Communication during the flight was very limited; there was no intercom or telephone, only hand signals or shouting above the roar of the engines. Contact between the planes of the squadron took place by light signals and there were several pathfinders in specially coloured planes flying in front of the flight. Firing different coloured signals they could transmit a new heading or the cancellation of the raid. The lack of radio on board led to two or three pigeons accompanying each plane on its way to England. In the case of a crash they would fly back to base with a note from the crew informing what had happened to them.

Adolf Genth (left) pictured with his flying partner in KAGOHL III, Radke. Thomas Genth

The bombers had to fly high to avoid AA guns and British aircraft and could reach 18,000 feet, though 16,000 feet was the normal flying height during the earlier raids by machines produced directly by Gotha.

The later planes built by Siemens-Schuckert and Luft Verkehrs GmbH were of poorer quality and flew at around 12,500 feet. Because of their heavy weight the planes could only reach a maximum speed of 80mph. During windy weather this would be reduced to 50mph, which was still more than a match for their British counterparts. Yet it was to be the weather, something the Germans could not accurately forecast due to depressions arriving from the Atlantic, that would ultimately decide the objectives and eventual success of a raid.

London was to be approached from the north-west using Epping Forest as a guide after a course was set for Foulness, easily identified from the North Sea. The bombers were to fly in a tight formation, usually a diamond-shape, to ensure a close defensive system. However, they would open out into different wings when the need arose, such as during intense AA fire.

Adolf Genth as a young soldier.
Thomas Genth

In April 1917 the Gothas were moved to the relative safety of Melle-Gontrode and St Denis-Westrem, but the large number of engine failures experienced by the planes continued to delay the commencement of the raids. The time was used to further train the crews, and modify the engines with new bearings, improved fuel pipe work, and reserve fuel tanks. However they still remained temperamental and 12 per cent of all flights had to be aborted.

By mid-May 1917 everything was at last in place and Brandenburg felt the time had come. On 18 May the squadron moved to the intermediate landing field at Nieuwmunster. However, a frustrating period of bad weather forced the Gothas to return to their bases, and the British, at last realizing the threat the planes might cause, unsuccessfully attacked St Denis-Westrem. Then on Friday, 25 May 1917 the weather at last turned favourable.

Gothas refuelling and preparing for take-off at Nieuwmunster for the Folkestone raid of 25 May 1917. Thomas Genth

Chapter Five

PRELUDE TO THE
BIG BANG

THE EARLIER EVENTS OF THE GOTHA RAID, FRIDAY, 25 MAY 1917

The aborted attack on London and flight along the railway to the coast

Twenty-three Gothas, one with Adolf Genth on board, took off at about 2.00 pm from St Denis-Westrem and Melle-Gontrode, but one soon had to abort with engine trouble. After a refuelling stop at Nieuwmunster they began flying over the sea at 3.30 pm at a height of 10,000 feet with Brandenburg leading the formation in a diamond-shaped phalanx. Another plane had to drop off with engine trouble and limped back to Belgium, leaving 21 planes to pass the Tongue Lightship off the North Kent coast at around 4.45 pm. The lightship immediately telephoned a warning that was passed to the Admiralty, yet the London warning controller failed to receive the message for another 15 minutes.

As the Gothas approached the Essex coast the formation split into two for defensive purposes and crossed the coastline between the rivers Blackwater and Crouch at an increased height of 16,000 feet. A single round was fired from the anti-aircraft battery at Highland Farm, Burnham-upon-Crouch, at 5.15 pm, but had no effect. Over 20 planes were rallied from RNAS bases at Manston, Westgate and Felixstowe, but by the time their elderly

The Gotha squadron at St Denis-Westrem before take-off on 25 May 1917.

Thomas Genth

Gotha GIV 405/16, commanded by Oberleutnant *Hans-Ulrich von Trotha, overhead the Belgian countryside heading west, possibly on the Folkestone raid of 25 May 1917. For von Trotha the war was to end on 19 June 1917 when his plane crashed and he was killed.* Thomas Genth

BE-type machines had reached their maximum height of 13,000 feet the enemy were long gone.

Yet as the Gothas swung around towards London they found the capital under a dense layer of cloud up to 7,000 feet and any thoughts of bombing it appeared to be out of the question (though it was not realized the capital's AA guns had been silenced by the earlier order). From their lofty position it could be seen the cloud petered out towards the south coast and at 5.30 pm Brandenburg signalled to his squadron to turn south into Kent over Gravesend. After continuing to fly south for a short time, Brandenburg ordered the planes to swing round to follow the South Eastern and Chatham's main (and almost straight) railway line to the Channel ports.

Using the cloud as cover, and as a result totally disorientating the home forces that expected them over London, the Gothas were hidden from view until they reappeared at Wrotham, west of Maidstone. The first four bombs of the raid were harmlessly dropped at 5.45 pm on Luddesdown and Harvel, including one that did not explode, though it later injured an officer examining it. Another fell at Linton, south of Maidstone, and four more landed close to the railway at Marden, killing a sheep. Further down the line ten bombs fell in the vicinity of Pluckley, Smarden and Bethersden, half of which failed to explode, while another exploded in the air. No damage was caused despite one bomb exploding within 10 feet of Smarden Rectory.

The bombers then reached Ashford, the railway centre of Kent, where unsurprisingly the extensive rail works were targeted. Six bombs were dropped, but they all missed the works; two falling near Bond Road, two on Providence Street and one each at Rugby Gardens and Beaver Green. One of the bombs heading for Providence Street exploded 40 feet in the air, causing the first fatality of the raid when 18-year-old Gladys Sparkes was killed. In addition two men, James Hook and Thomas Brooke, and a boy, Ernest Burden, were injured. Another bomb failed to explode, while two others fell harmlessly into fields and allotments.

Continuing eastwards towards the coast, the northern wing of the Gothas dropped four bombs at Kingsnorth, Shadoxhurst and Mersham, killing a sheep. The southern wing took aim at the Royal Military Canal with one dud landing at a field at Ruckinge and five falling on Bilsington, one landing in an open grave in the churchyard but failing to explode. An unarmed Bristol F26 fighter, piloted by Flight Lieutenant Baker, was encountered and attacked, forcing it to head for Lympne Airfield. The hapless Baker had just landed when the airfield itself was attacked with three 50kg and nineteen 12½kg bombs. Two fell without effect near a hangar, another in a quarry to the east of the aerodrome and a third burst 400 feet in the air. The others landed in the centre of the airfield, yet very little damage was caused and there were no casualties. Flight Lieutenant Gerald Gathergood scrambled one DH5 fighter; however, it would take him a good 20 minutes to reach the height of the Gothas.

After leaving Lympne a single bomb was dropped 100 yards from the eastern end of Sandling Tunnel on the main line, but failed to explode. Continuing east the ancient Cinque Port of Hythe lay next in the bombers' path.

The attack on Hythe

Sixteen bombs (seven 50kg and nine 12½kg) were dropped on Hythe, causing two fatalities. Three of the bombs failed to explode, two of them dropping through houses in Cobden Road and West Parade, while seven fell on the beach and in gardens and allotments, injuring one man. Another fell harmlessly on Hythe Golf Course and one exploded above the Metropole Steam Laundry, where splinters penetrated the roof, fortunately without anyone being hurt. The deaths were caused by a bomb that fell in the parish churchyard, killing Daniel Stringer Lyth, and two that burst in the air, shrapnel from one fatally injuring Amy Parker. The final two bombs fell on rough ground and the Imperial Hotel Golf Course close to the Royal Military Canal.

The RFC School of Aerial Gunnery was surprisingly not attacked and because they were trainees the pilots were unable to scramble any of their planes. After the raid this led to some hostility from townsfolk, who branded the pilots useless, and bricks were reported to have been thrown at them.

Mr Lyth was verger of Hythe Parish Church and a former Town Sergeant. He was killed by a bomb splinter that ripped into his right thigh while standing at the west door of the church. He had been engaged in conversation with the Vicar, Revd H D Dale, and his wife inside the church when they heard the explosions outside. As they went to investigate, a bomb fell in the churchyard shattering tombstones and sending shrapnel in all directions. The Vicar was saved from injury by a tin of throat lozenges in his coat pocket that deflected a piece of shrapnel, though his wife was injured in the face. Mrs Parker, of Ormonde Road, was killed by a bomb splinter that entered her shoulder when she went outside to call her child indoors. Two further people, Emily and Jane Nicholls, of 12 Albert Road, were injured.

Continuing to hug the coast, the raiders flew eastwards, the northern flank attacking Shorncliffe Camp (defended only by small AA guns atop the Napoleonic Martello towers) and Cheriton, and the southern flank attacking Sandgate.

The attack on Sandgate

Sandgate fotunately suffered little damage and no fatalities from the five bombs dropped on the seaside village. Two of the bombs exploded on waste ground close to the coastguard station, causing no damage, while equally ineffectual was a bomb that fell in Coolinge Lane. Another shattered the windows of Enbrook Manor and the fifth bomb landed in the Enbrook Stream opposite the Fleur de Lys pub, hurling large stones across the road into the properties opposite.

The attack on Shorncliffe Army Camp and the military casualties

Six 50kg and 21kg bombs were dropped on Shorncliffe Army Camp and Cheriton by the northern flank of the Gothas. One of them exploded amongst a line of

The Cavalry Training Ground, Shorncliffe Camp in the early years of the twentieth century. In the background can be seen Royal Military Avenue, where bombs fell in the Folkestone raid and one person was killed. Peter and Annie Bamford

Canadian infantrymen on the howitzer lines preparing for a march, killing eleven men of the Central and Western Ontario regiments. Another killed four Canadian gunners, along with an American fighting in the Canadian Army, pitching a tent on Risboro' Field: it was reported their blown-apart bodies had to be gathered up in bags. A further Canadian casualty was caused by an unexploded bomb that fell on the cavalry drill ground and a British soldier was killed by a bomb that hit a tent in the quarantine quarters. The other bombs fell at these locations at the camp:

one close to the Military Hospital (dud)
one south-west of No. 9 Martello tower (dud)
one on the tailor's shop in the Canadian 8th Battalion's lines (25 injured)
one on the Canadian ASC lines
one 20 yards south of the tailor's shop (dud)
three in the garden of Underhill House
one near the road at Lower St Martin's Plain
two at Lower Dibgate
one on Dibgate Plain
one on the roof of the WC in the Officer's Mess of the Canadian Headquarters, Napier Barracks (however, the sturdy concrete roof ensured only a small hole was blown in it).

The 18 military fatalities, all buried at Shorncliffe Military Cemetery, were:

ARBUCKLE, Bert, Age 38.
Gunner 2085324 Reserve Brigade, Canadian Field Artillery.
Son of Riley and Lucinda Arbuckle of Indiana, USA. Fatally injured while pitching a tent on Risboro' Field, Shorncliffe Camp, died in Shorncliffe Military Hospital on 26 May 1917.
Buried in Shorncliffe Military Cemetery Grave No. S.538.

BROWN, W, Age 21.
Gunner 342862 Reserve Brigade, Canadian Field Artillery.
Killed while pitching a tent on Risboro' Field, Shorncliffe Camp.
Buried in Shorncliffe Military Cemetery Grave No. T.551 on 28 May 1917.

BRUCE, James Alexander, Age 21.
Gunner 2085320 Reserve Brigade, Canadian Field Artillery.
Son of D S and C Bruce of 56 Second Street, St Lambert, Quebec.
Killed while pitching a tent on Risboro' Field, Shorncliffe Camp.
Buried in Shorncliffe Military Cemetery Grave No. T.545 on 28 May 1917.

DESALEUX, Jules Benjamin Alfred, Age 29.
Gunner 1250216 76 Battery Reserve Brigade, Canadian Field Artillery.
Son of J B A and Edith Desaleux of London, husband of Alice E Desaleux of 1399 Winnipeg Avenue, Winnipeg, Manitoba.
Killed while pitching a tent on Risboro' Field, Shorncliffe Camp.
Buried in Shorncliffe Military Cemetery Grave No. R.540 on 28 May 1917.
DOIG, Arthur, Age 24

Lance Corporal 922065 200th Battalion, Canadian Infantry (Central Ontario Regiment).
Son of Andrew and Maggie Murray Doig of Birtle, Manitoba.
Killed while preparing for a march on the howitzer lines, Shorncliffe Camp.
Buried in Shorncliffe Military Cemetery Grave No. T.546 on 28 May 1917.

JENNER, Oron Alfred, Age 26,
Company Quartermaster Serjeant 273124 3rd Reserve Battalion, Canadian Infantry (Central Ontario Regiment).
The only son of Elizabeth Catherine Jenner of 32 Redpath Avenue, Toronto, Ontario.
Embarked from Halifax on 18 April 1917 and disembarked from the SS *Scandinavian* at Liverpool on 29 April 1917. The next day he was stationed with the 3rd Canadian Reserve Battalion at Sandling, near Hythe, before being transferred to Shorncliffe Camp.
Killed while preparing for a march on the howitzer lines, Shorncliffe Camp.
Buried in Shorncliffe Military Cemetery Grave No. T.554 on 28 May 1917.

McARTHUR, J, Age 21
Private 922562 200th Battalion, Canadian Infantry (Central Ontario Regiment).
Killed while preparing for a march on the howitzer lines, Shorncliffe Camp.
Buried in Shorncliffe Military Cemetery Grave No. T.547 on 28 May 1917.

MacDONALD, R, Age 19
Private 922836 200th Battalion, Canadian Infantry (Central Ontario Regiment).
Son of John I and Sarah MacDonald of Basswood, Manitoba.
Killed while preparing for a march on the howitzer lines, Shorncliffe Camp.
Buried in Shorncliffe Military Cemetery Grave No. T.553 on 28 May 1917.

McNAIR, H, Age 20
Private 922225 200th Battalion, Canadian Infantry (Central Ontario Regiment)
Killed while preparing for a march on the howitzer lines, Shorncliffe Camp.
Buried in Shorncliffe Military Cemetery Grave No. T.550 on 28 May 1917.

McNULTY, James D, Age 25
Gunner 1251128 Reserve Brigade, Canadian Field Artillery.
Son of Patrick and Margaret Coleman McNulty of Suite 35, Arlington Apartments, Edmonton, Alberta. Born in Valley City, North Dakota, USA.
Killed while pitching a tent on Risboro' Field, Shorncliffe Camp.
Buried in Shorncliffe Military Cemetery Grave No. R.539 on 28 May 1917.

MARSHALL, Charles, Age 23
Private 875420 184th Battalion, Canadian Infantry (Western Ontario Regiment).
Fatally injured while preparing for a march on the howitzer lines, Shorncliffe Camp, died on 26 May 1917.
Buried in Shorncliffe Military Cemetery Grave No. T.552 on 28 May 1917.

MERCHANT, A W, Age 34
Private 875090 184th Battalion, Canadian Infantry, (Western Ontario Regiment).
Husband of L E Merchant of 178 Kermedy Street, Winnipeg, Manitoba.
Killed while preparing for a march on the howitzer lines, Shorncliffe Camp.
Buried in Shorncliffe Military Cemetery Grave No. R.543 on 28 May 1917.

MILLER, John, Age 41
Private 202316 2nd/4th Battalion, South Lancashire Regiment.
Son of Mrs Agnes Shaw.
Killed in the Quarantine Quarters, Shorncliffe Camp.
Buried in Shorncliffe Military Cemetery Grave No. C.556 on 29 May 1917.

PADLEY, F, Age 24
Private 922556 200th Battalion, Canadian Infantry (Central Ontario Regiment).
Son of Harry and Elizabeth Padley of 58 Church Drive, Carrington, Nottingham, England.
Killed while preparing for a march on the howitzer lines, Shorncliffe Camp.
Buried in Shorncliffe Military Cemetery Grave No. R.542 on 28 May 1917.

PELLUET, R, Age 25
Private 922514 200th Battalion, Canadian Infantry (Central Ontario Regiment).
Killed while preparing for a march on the howitzer lines, Shorncliffe Camp.
Buried in Shorncliffe Military Cemetery No. R.544 on 28 May 1917.

SUTHERLAND, Jack, Age 31
Private 922299 200th Battalion, Canadian Infantry (Central Ontario Regiment).
Son of Alexander and Elizabeth Sutherland of Bradford, Ontario.
Killed while preparing for a march on the howitzer lines, Shorncliffe Camp.
Buried in Shorncliffe Military Cemetery Grave No. T.549 on 28 May 1917.

TENNYSON, Ernest, Age unknown
Private 922331 200th Battalion, Canadian Infantry (Central Ontario Regiment).
Killed while preparing for a march on the howitzer lines, Shorncliffe Camp.
Buried in Shorncliffe Military Cemetery Grave No. T.548 on 28 May 1917.

YEO, L G, Age unknown.
Private 226191 Canadian Reserve Cavalry Regiment.
Killed by an unexploded bomb on the Cavalry Drill Ground.
Buried in Shorncliffe Military Cemetery Grave No. R.541 on 28 May 1917.

In recognition of the tremendous sacrifices made by the Canadian Army, around 1,500 local schoolchildren gathered at Shorncliffe Military Cemetery during a ceremony on Wednesday, 13 June 1917 to lay flowers on the graves of those who had been killed. Two Canadian officers and the Mayors of Folkestone and Hythe made speeches and the Band of the Canadian Artillery played 'The Maple Leaf' and 'God Save the King'. 'Canadian Flower Day', as it was known, became an annual event and in succeeding years around 3,000 schoolchildren attended, along

Canadian Flower Day at Shorncliffe Military Cemetery c.1920. Peter and Annie Bamford

with local dignitaries and representatives from Canada, including the Canadian High Commissioner. Since the Second World War the service has become more low-key, but happily, is still supported by local schoolchildren. The cemetery, where 296 Canadian soldiers lie, remains an oasis of tranquillity with superb views of the Seabrook Valley and Hythe Bay.

The attack on Cheriton

In the residential area of Cheriton, situated to the north and east of Shorncliffe Camp, a number of bombs were aimed at the main London-Dover railway line, which ran through this fast-rising suburb of Folkestone. However, they all fell short and landed mainly to the south of the line in an area between Horn Street and Risborough Lane. Three bombs fell in allotments near Horn Street, while another landed in the back garden of 52 Royal Military Avenue, killing 54-year-old Alfred Down. The worst-hit area was Oaks Road, just off Risborough Lane, where three bombs landed killing 16-year-old Dorothy Burgin and 5-year-old Francis Considine.

Chapter Six

THE INNOCENTS AWAKE

THE ATTACK ON FOLKESTONE, 25 MAY 1917

Folkestone laid bare

As the Gothas flew eastwards into Folkestone they came across a town that, despite its large military presence, was woefully unprepared for an enemy attack by air. There was no air-raid warning system, and even if there had been it would not have sounded; the local authorities had not been warned of any attack by the London warning control centre who presumably had no idea where the Gothas actually were. Furthermore, there were no AA guns in the Folkestone area; the nearest were the six army shore batteries around Dover, who only spotted the planes once the raid on Folkestone was almost over. Though each gun was capable, if the crew could determine the aim of angles and height required, of firing at aircraft up to 20,000 feet high, they were targeted to repel attacks from the sea.

A pleasant, sunny, spring evening had enticed many to venture out into the streets of Folkestone. It was payday and the shops in the High Street and Tontine Street were busy supplying their customers with goods for the Whitsun weekend. Some had taken advantage of the warm weather to enjoy a stroll along the Leas, or play a game of tennis in the grounds of one of the many private schools in the West End.

Just after 6.00 pm a number of distant explosions were heard that gradually increased in volume. However, no one was unduly alarmed, suspecting they were

The down-side approach road to Folkestone Central Station, where Edward Horn was killed, pictured shortly after the raid. Folkestone Library

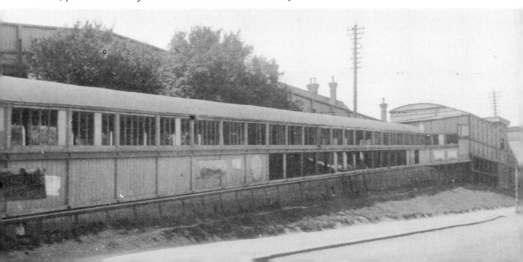

the sounds of training exercises at Shorncliffe Camp. The Gothas flew into the town with Brandenburg at their head at a height of around 14,000 feet over a screen of clouds and as the noise of their engines grew louder they were spotted in the West End. The initial impression that they were friendly aircraft proved to be sadly mistaken as the bombs began to fall.

The West End and Central Station areas

Eighteen bombs fell in this area
Kilkenny Crescent/Turketel Road: 1 dud
Grimston Gardens: 1
Shorncliffe Road area: 3 (2 duds). Two killed
Jointon Road/Trinity Road: 2 (1 dud). One killed
Radnor Park West: 2
Central Station area (including Cheriton Road and Kingsnorth Gardens): 9 (7 duds). One killed

The formation of the Gothas moved closer together over Folkestone as they continued to hug the line of the railway. The first bomb to fall on Folkestone was a dud that landed at the junction of Kilkenny Crescent and Turketel Road and another fell in nearby Grimston Gardens, causing a large crater in a lawn-tennis court. Three bombs fell in the vicinity of Shorncliffe Road, two of them at the back of Abbotsfield School. Flying shrapnel from one of these bombs claimed the first two Folkestone fatalities of the raid in Miss Doris Walton, who was playing tennis in the grounds of Athelstan School, and Albert Castle, a gardener at Grange School. Two bombs landed in the Jointon Road area. One fell on the pavement outside 'Kimberley', the residence of Dr W J Tyson, killing pedestrian Maggie Bartleet, and the other buried itself in the grounds of the Pleasure Gardens Theatre, but failed to explode. Mrs Ewart Potter, the wife of the theatre's manager, and her young daughter Jill were at the time only 30 feet from where the bomb fell, and were fortunate it was a dud. Soldiers subsequently removed the bomb. Close to Folkestone Central railway station, two bombs fell on the west side of Radnor Park, but it was obviously the station itself that the Gothas were targeting. Nine bombs fell either side of it, of which an incredible seven were duds, but unfortunately one did explode in the down-side approach road killing Edward Horn, butler to Sir Thomas Devitt of Radnor Cliff, and two horses. Three of the bombs intended for the station fell in Kingsnorth Gardens. One went through a house and fell on a cot from which a child had been lifted a few moments previously and another penetrated the ground to a depth of 16 feet and travelled laterally for another 16 feet before rising another 10 feet towards the ground!

Radnor Park and Foord areas

Six bombs fell in this area
Wiltie Gardens (Nos. 2 and 4): 1
Radnor Park Crescent (No. 46): 1
Bournemouth Gardens (No. 2): 1
Boscombe Road (No. 18): 1
St John's Church Road (No. 3): 1
Corner of Foord Road and Radnor Park Road: 1. One killed

Beyond the Central Station further bombs were aimed at the railway line. However, they were all wide of the mark and it was particularly fortunate that the great 19-arch brick viaduct crossing the Foord Valley was not hit. Damage to the viaduct would have halted all rail traffic to Folkestone Harbour, the line to Dover having been closed due to a landslide in the Warren in December 1915.

The six bombs aimed at the railway in this area fell among residential streets, causing one fatality. One bomb damaged Nos. 2 and 4 Wiltie Gardens, while another did the same to 46 Radnor Park Crescent. The bomb dropped on Bournemouth Gardens fell into the forecourt of No. 2, home to builder Mr Crosswell, and brought the front of the house crashing down; fortunately all the family were in the back of the house and escaped harm. Mr G Salmon and his family at 3 St John's Church Road also had a narrow escape when a bomb fell into the back of their premises, smashing the brickwork. The sixth bomb fell behind advertising hoardings on the corner of Foord Road and Radnor Park Road, the old spa site opposite the Castle Inn, killing coal carter George Butcher and injuring Charles Savage.

The corner of Foord Road and Radnor Park Road, where George Butcher was killed. Behind the gate can be seen damage to the advertising hoardings and pockmarks to the wall. Folkestone Library

Bouverie Road East area
Eight bombs fell in this area
Osborne Hotel, corner of Bouverie Road West and Christchurch Road: 1
Manor Road (Nos. 21 and 22): 2. One killed
Bouverie Square (No. 14): 1
Cheriton Gardens (rear): 1
Bouverie Road East (Nos. 19 and 21): 2 (1 dud). Five killed
Millfield (No. 1): 1

Away from the railway line, the Bouverie Road area of central Folkestone was targeted and suffered badly. Standing on the corner of Bouverie Road West and Christchurch Road, the Osborne Hotel was severely damaged when a bomb fell through the roof and ploughed its way down to the basement before exploding. A gas main was ignited and burned merrily on a pile of broken furniture, yet remarkably none of the hotel's guests were hurt (fortunately, many had already

The wrecked Osborne Hotel on the corner of Bouverie Road West and Christchurch Road, pictured shortly after the raid of 25 May 1917. Folkestone Library

evacuated the building). A number of properties nearby had their windows smashed, and the house of Mr F W Pepper, whose horse was killed in the raid by a bomb dropped behind Grove Road, was struck by shrapnel.

The rear of West Lodge, 21 Manor Road before the raid. Marlinova Collection

In nearby Manor Road a bomb scored a direct hit on West Lodge, 21 Manor Road, causing the greater part of the building to collapse. Buried in the basement under a mound of rubble was the cook, Jane Marshment, whose lifeless body could not be recovered until 24 hours later, because of the amount of masonry that had to be cleared. Another servant who was in the house when the raid commenced became frightened by the noise and ran across the road to another house, the bomb falling on No. 21 almost as soon as she left it. Across the road a further bomb fell in the back garden of Dr Percy Lewis's premises at

The front of West Lodge after the raid. One person was killed and the building so badly damaged it had to be demolished. From the book *Folkestone During the War 1914-1919*

No. 22. The back of the house was wrecked and a piano was smashed up, along with a carved chest and other furniture.

Christchurch School in Bouverie Road East was badly damaged when a bomb

The rear of Christchurch School, damaged by a bomb that fell behind 14 Bouverie Square, with the damaged roof of Nos. 19 and 21 Bouverie Road East in the background. The photograph was taken soon after the raid. Folkestone Library

fell behind 14 Bouverie Square, breaking every window and wrecking the interior. The school was declared unfit for use and its girl pupils were temporarily accommodated at the Technical Institute on Grace Hill. Two more bombs damaged Millfield Lodge at No. 1 Millfield and Frederic Hall solicitors in Cheriton Gardens.

A bomb that fell outside Nos. 19 and 21 Bouverie Road East, however, caused the greatest devastation in this area; wrecking both buildings and killing five people. Mr John Burke, who ran a boot- and shoe-repair shop at No. 21, was killed when the bomb threw him across the road into the railings of the County School for Girls. Chambermaid Miss Kathleen Chapman was walking in company with soldier George Bloodworth on her way to collect a pair of shoes from Mr Burke's shop when shrapnel from the bomb mortally wounded them both. Harold Banks was waiting for a friend when the bomb fell just 10 yards from him. He later died from shock in hospital, as did May Arnold, the proprietor of

The shattered frontage of No. 21 Bouverie Road East, where John Burke was killed. Peter and Annie Bamford

the café at No. 19, who was inside the building when the front walls were completely blown in. The basements of Nos. 19 and 21 were said to have presented a scene of indescribable wreckage with broken furniture, bedsteads, bedding and stores of all kinds entangled with the punctured ends of gas and water pipes and the torn remains of electric wires.

The unexploded bomb that fell in Bouverie Road East shattered the frontage of Durban's butcher's shop at No. 11. One of the assistants, Horace Brooman, was injured in the head and taken to hospital and three lady assistants suffered minor injuries.

A very rare view of Stokes shop in 1907 with partners George and William Stokes and some of their staff. The shop was blown apart by the Tontine Street bomb and William Stokes was killed. Mrs Howard

Tontine Street

2 bombs fell in this area
Tontine Street: 1. Sixty-one killed
High Street (rear): 1 (dud)

Sadly, the carnage in Bouverie Road East proved to be just the prelude to a far greater tragedy in Folkestone's main shopping area, Tontine Street, when a single bomb killed 61 persons in the most horrific manner.

A sizeable queue had formed outside Messrs Stokes's greengrocery store at Nos. 51a-c after word had got round they had received a consignment of precious potatoes. The majority of the queue were women; many of them accompanied by their small children, who were happily playing in the early-evening sunshine. One such queue was vividly described by Mrs C S Peel:

Anyone who penetrated the poor neighbourhoods became familiar with the queues of

women and children who waited outside the shabby shops common to the poor districts of all towns. They carried baskets, string bags, fish basses, bags made of American cloth and babies, and stood shifting their burdens from one arm to another to ease their aching backs. Yet often, in spite of cold, rain and weariness, there was a flow of wit. Sometimes a late-comer would try to sneak in at the head of the line and then there would be trouble, promptly allayed by the policeman or special constable. The middle classes who could not obtain servants also swelled the queues, though the rich escaped these unpleasant tasks, partly because they could send servants to shop for them and partly because the customer who brought on a large scale could still have his goods delivered at his house.

The sound of explosions in other parts of the town had led some people in the street to take cover in shop doorways, yet the majority continued with their shopping. Then at 6.22 pm disaster struck. In an instant, and without warning, a bomb from one of the Gothas exploded outside the shop, sending the roof crashing down on the people inside and filling the top part of the street with the most truly dreadful scene imaginable. A total of 44 people were killed instantly and a further 17 later died in local hospitals, their bodies blown apart by the terrific force of the explosion. Severed heads and limbs, mangled horse-carcasses and rubble from the wrecked shop lay about the street, while a huge sheet of flame from a fractured gas

On the other side of the road from Stokes's shop, Franks' plumbers and decorators and Gosnold Bros' drapers suffered blast damage from the bomb. Marlinova Collection

The damaged Tontine Toilet Salon/Premium Trading Stamp Co. building at No. 64, seconds after the preceding picture was taken (notice the lady with the pram in both views). Peter and Annie Bamford

main shot out from the pavement. Mr Harry Reeve, Chief Constable of Folkestone Police, summed it up by saying it was the most appalling sight he had ever seen, the memory of which would remain with him to his dying day.

Mrs Adelaide Moore, a member of the St John Ambulance, was amongst those who later received a Silver Medal for attending to the dead and injured. She was shopping in Gosnold's drapery store opposite Stokes's when the bomb fell and, despite receiving severe head injuries, attended to the shop owner George Gosnold and dressed a bad wound in his right side. She remained with him until he was conveyed to the Royal Victoria Hospital, and then attended to more of the wounded before she was herself taken to the hospital.

Many Folkestone families lost loved ones. Mr Harry Beer lost his two young sons, Arthur and William, and had to inform his brother fighting at the Front that his wife and daughter had been killed in the most frightful way; the face of little Annie Beer (2), for example, was just blown away. Sisters Gertrude (12) and Mabel (9) Bowbrick lost their lives, and their mother, Nellie, was seriously injured. Mr Fred Holloway of 13 Burrow Road also lost his two little girls, nine-year-old Mary, and Veronica, who was only sixteen months old, while Alfred Norris of 30 Black Bull Road lost all three members of his family: wife Florence (24), little Florrie (2) and baby Willie (10 months). Florrie was the apple of her father's eye, with her golden curls, and how he must have suffered knowing his darling daughter's head had been severed from her little body. Dorothy Jackman (14) of 12 Connaught Road was happily talking and laughing with her two friends Gwennie Terry (13) and

Madge McDonald (22) when the bomb struck the pavement just a few yards away. Miss Jackman and Miss Terry were killed at once and Miss McDonald suffered appalling injuries that led to her death on 2 June.

Among the three Belgians killed was Marie Snoawert, who finally succumbed to her injuries a month after the raid. She lived with a group of Belgian refugees at 7 Copthall Gardens and was in the company of three of them as they queued up for potatoes outside Stokes's shop. Miss Snoawert's companions all received horrific injuries from the blast, but fortunately survived. An estimated eight or nine people who were sheltering in the doorway of Gosnold's were reported to have been killed.

From out of town, Nellie Feist (50) of Coombe Farm, Hawkinge, in company with her grandson Stanley (5) and Albert Daniels (12), was passing up Tontine Street on her way home when the bomb fell. All three were found dead in their cart next to the mangled remains of their horse.

In Stokes's shop, proprietor William Stokes (46) and his son Arthur (14), along

A crowd gathers shortly after the Folkestone raid to view the site in Tontine Street where the fatal bomb dropped. Peter and Annie Bamford

with bookkeepers Edith Eales (17) and Florrie Rumsey (17), suffered appalling injuries, from which they never recovered. The shop was destroyed, though it was quickly rebuilt and the family business carried on for many years. Countless other shops were damaged in the area from No. 35 to the Congregational Church, where the clock stopped at 6.22 pm. Among the shops that suffered damage were:

West Side

No. 35 Henry Warren, fruiterer and greengrocer

No. 37 Messrs Murdoch's Piano and Music Saloon (plate-glass window fell into the street)

No. 39 D Swift, Cabin Café

No. 41 William Whittingstall, fruiterer and greengrocer

No. 43 J A Balmford, chemist (the shop window was blown in. Mr Balmford attended to several of the wounded)

No. 45-47 Dunk, builder (frontage damaged by shrapnel)

No. 49 Mackeson's wine and spirit merchants (windows broken and stock destroyed)

No. 49a Ernest Lambrini, tobacconist and hairdresser (front of shop badly damaged)

No. 49b Gosnold Bros, drapers (windows blown out and shop badly damaged)

No. 51 John Waite, confectioner (shopfront badly damaged and Mr Waite was wounded in the back of the head by shrapnel)

No. 51a-c Stokes Bros, fruiterers and greengrocers (shop totally destroyed with owner William Stokes and his son Arthur fatally injured and Frederick Stokes badly injured. Bookkeepers Edith Eales and Florrie Rumsey were also fatally injured)

No. 53 Brewery Tap pub (roof and windows damaged)

No. 55 John Jones, fruiterer and confectioner (Councillor Jones received a nasty wound in his leg)

No. 57 Arcadia Bazaar

No. 59 Henry Saunders, bootmaker

No. 61 W O Smith, tobacconist

No. 63 Gosnold Bros

No. 65 Morris Beef Co.

No. 67 William Perry, grocer

No. 69 Frank Palmer, outfitter

No. 71 Timothy Whites (Mr W B Metcalfe and his wife attended to the injured with lint, splints and bandages from the shop. Phyllis Cooper, who was dreadfully injured, was amongst those treated by the couple, but she later died)

No. 73-79 R G Wood, outfitters (sustained frontal damage)

East Side

No. 34-36 Ernest Lambrini, hairdresser

No. 38 Post Office

No. 40 Durban, butcher's

No. 42 Domestic Bazaar Co.

No. 44 Electricity substation

No. 46 C Wakely, confectioner

Work begins on reconstructing Stokes's shop while a group of inquisitive children look on. From the book Folkestone During the War 1914-1919

No. 48-52 Dunk, builder

No. 54 Biago Rossi, confectioner

No. 56-60 Gosnold Bros, draper (shopfront and interior badly damaged. A number of people inside, and sheltering in the shop doorway, were killed)

No. 62 W J Franks, plumber and decorator (frontage damaged)

No. 64 Tontine Toilet Salon/The Premium Trading Stamp Co. Ltd (frontage damaged)

No. 68 William Hall, pork butcher (Mr Hall was killed)

No. 70-72 John P Marsh, draper

No. 74 Francis Reich, silversmith (Mr Reich was injured)

Windows of houses in St Michael's Street, Mill Bay, Payer's Park and the High Street were shattered. Another bomb fell near Payer's store at the rear of the High Street, but failed to explode.

East Folkestone

6* bombs fell in this area

St John's Street: 1 (*plus an unrecorded dud later dug up in 1932)

Grove Road (rear): 2

Folly Road Crossing: 1

East Cliff: 2 (1 dud)

The bombers continued east following the line of the railway. One bomb just missed the line and partially destroyed Nos. 24-30 St John's Street (later renumbered 26-32). Worst hit was No. 28, where the roof was torn off and the ceiling collapsed on bedridden Lily Coleman (79) and a child, Hilda Chittenden. In

The damage to Nos. 26-30 St John's Street caused by the Gotha raid of 25 May 1917. Peter and Annie Bamford

No. 26 John Clark was injured.

Two further bombs also just missed the railway and fell behind houses in Grove Road, killing a horse belonging to F W Pepper, whose house in Bouverie Road West was also damaged in the raid. A number of windows in the Junction Station area around Folly Road, Tram Road and Warren Road were shattered by either a bomb or an anti-aircraft shell fired from Dover.

The Gothas flew into the town from the west in their usual closely spaced two-wing attack. A total of 51 bombs were dropped on Folkestone in ten minutes, of which 20 were duds (6 of these fell harmlessly into the sea). There were twenty-one 50kg bombs and thirty 12½kg; not of a particularly large calibre, but some of the shells were of the aerial torpedo variety and fiercely explosive (such as the one that fell on Tontine Street). A further unrecorded dud was discovered at St John's Street in 1932. The five bombs not indicated on the map (having fallen on the outskirts of the town) landed at Enbrook, the west side of Coolinge Lane (in the grounds of a school) and three on or around the golf links.

A map showing where the bombs fell

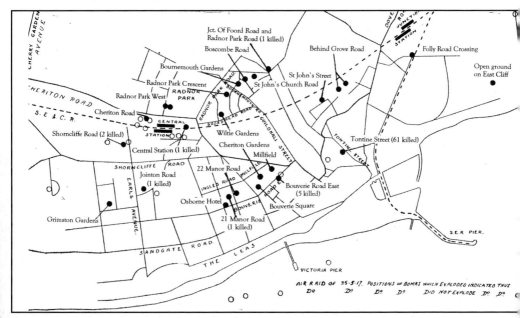

Chapter Seven

THE INNOCENTS ASLEEP

THE VICTIMS OF THE GOTHA AIR RAID, 25 MAY 1917

Hospitals and the death-toll

Local medical units and the police expediently carried out the very grim and melancholy task of removing the bodies and remains of the deceased to the mortuaries in the area, where relatives faced the most distressing task of identifying their loved ones from a few mangled remains. Over 80 injured persons, many piled onto the back of carts or, in the case of small children, carried all the way, were taken to the Royal Victoria Hospital, where they were huddled in corridors because of the lack of space. The book *Folkestone During the War 1914-1919* described the scene at the hospital:

> *Those who were in the hospital on that fateful night of 25th May will never forget the grim sight of the bodies huddled together in the corridor, and the limbs brought in wrapped in blankets. It was more terrible than a battle scene. It was so ruthless and wanton in its savagery. There were the bodies of women and children, maimed and*

The Royal Victoria Hospital as it looked during the First World War. The majority of the casualties from the Folkestone raid were taken there. Marlinova Collection

shattered by the crime of war. The moans of the sufferers were heard in every part of the building.

The RVH soon became overloaded with the dead, dying and injured, and other victims were taken to Shorncliffe Military Hospital and the Canadian Eye and Ear Hospital in the converted West Cliff Hotel. However, they too became full and some of the wounded were transferred to hospitals outside the borough.

Extensive research through local papers of the time, as well as mortuary and cemetery records, has revealed the final civilian death-toll of the raid to be 78. Folkestone suffered 72 fatalities (16 men, 29 women and 27 children), Cheriton 3 (1 man and 2 children), Hythe 2 (1 man and 1 woman) and Ashford 1 (a woman). This was the highest number of British civilian dead caused by any air raid in the First World War up to that point and it was to be passed only once; on 13 June 1917 when 158 civilians and 4 soldiers were killed in Essex and the East End of London. A greater number of military casualties occurred during a raid on Sheerness and Chatham on 3 September 1917 when 133 were killed (one a civilian), 132 of them by a bomb that fell on the drill hall at Chatham's Royal Naval Barracks. The hall was being used as sleeping accommodation and, as it was night-time, was full. The high casualty rate was the result of flying splinters from the shattered glass roof.

The total number killed in the Kent raids was 336 (Chatham Dockyard 132, Folkestone 72, Dover 26, Ramsgate 25, Margate 18, Shorncliffe Camp 18, Sheerness 15, Otterpool Camp 15, Broadstairs 3, Cheriton 3, Hythe 2, Chatham 2, Gillingham 2, Deal and Walmer 2, Ashford 1).

Victims of the Folkestone raid were also taken to the Canadian Eye and Ear Hospital at the West Cliff Hotel. Marlinova Collection

The Shorncliffe Military Hospital received both military and civilian casualties from the Folkestone raid. Peter and Annie Bamford

The fatalities

(all in Folkestone except where mentioned)

ARNOLD, May Alexandra
Age: 21

ARNOLD, May Alexandra

Address: 19 Bouverie Road East, Folkestone. Fatally injured in Bouverie Road East, died on the same day from shock at Moore Barracks Hospital, Shorncliffe Camp. Buried in Shorncliffe Military Cemetery on 26 May 1917. The gravestone remains in good condition.

The widow of Bombardier F Arnold CFA, May was the proprietor of a café at 19 Bouverie Road East and was inside the building when a bomb fell just outside. She was hit by falling debris and was initially taken to the adjoining Bouverie Hotel before being transferred to hospital.

BANKS, Harold Hayward
Age: 25
Address: 20 Victoria Grove, Folkestone.
Fatally injured in Bouverie Road East, died at 11.45 am on 26 May 1917 from shock at Moore Barracks Hospital, Shorncliffe Camp. Buried in Cheriton Road Cemetery Section C1872 (c) on 30 May 1917. Gravestone not extant. Harold was a chauffeur who was waiting for a friend outside a barber's shop in Bouverie Road East when a bomb fell 10 yards away from him.

BARKER, Eliza Mary
Age: 33
Address: 29 Bradstone Road, Folkestone.
Fatally injured in the body in Tontine Street, died in the Royal Victoria Hospital that same night. Buried in Cheriton Road

BARKER, Eliza Mary

Cemetery Section C1870 (c) on 31 May 1917. The gravestone remains in good condition.

Eliza was the wife of Edward Horace Barker (35), a porter employed with Smith Furniture. She left a ten-year-old son who was looked after by an aunt. Soon after the raid Mr Barker appealed against conscription on the grounds of ill-health claiming he was blind in his right eye and had a bad heart. He was granted three months' temporary exemption.

BARTLEET, Maggie Gray
Age: 24
Address: 27 Connaught Road, Folkestone.
Fatally injured in Jointon Road from injuries to the head and body, pronounced dead upon arrival at the Royal Victoria Hospital. Buried in Cheriton Road Cemetery Section C1852 (c) on 29 May 1917. The inscription on the gravestone is now very faded. Known as 'Madge' and wife of Joseph Johnson Bartleet, Sergeant Major in the RAMC. Witnesses report that Mrs Bartleet's legs were blown out from under her after she had just crossed the junction of Jointon Road and Trinity Road.

BEER, Annie
Age: 30
Address: 90 Black Bull Road, Folkestone.
Died in Tontine Street from terrible wounds. Buried in Cheriton Road Cemetery Section C1868 (c) on 31 May 1917 with her daughter, who was also killed. The body was exhumed on

BEER, Annie

14 July 1917 by licence of the Home Secretary dated 3 July 1917 and re-interred on the same day in Section E6805B. The gravestone remains in good condition.

Annie was the mother of Annie Beer (2) and aunt of Arthur Beer (11) and William Beer (9), who were also killed in the raid when they were queuing with her to buy potatoes from Stokes's shop. Her husband, Ernest Beer, a marine fireman, who was on active service when she was killed, later remarried and always remained silent on the death of his first wife and daughter. Many of his friends never even realized he had been married before until after his death when a locket was found upon him with a picture of Annie inside.

BEER, Annie and BEER, Annie (Rosie)

BEER, Annie (Rosie)
Age: 2
Address: 90 Black Bull Road, Folkestone.
Died in Tontine Street when the whole of her face was blown away.
Buried in Cheriton Road Cemetery Section C5789 (c) on 31 May 1917 with her mother, who was also killed. The body was exhumed on 14 July 1917 by licence of the Home Secretary dated 3 July 1917 and re-interred on the same day in Section E6805A.

BEER, Annie 'Rosie'

Daughter of Annie Beer (30) and cousin of Arthur Beer (11) and William Beer (9), who were also killed in the raid. Little Annie, who was known by her family as 'Rosie', was sitting in a pram when the bomb fell, and was killed instantly.

BEER, Arthur Stephen
Age: 11
Address: 67 Bridge Street, Folkestone.
Died in Tontine Street from head, leg and chest injuries. Buried in Cheriton Road Cemetery Section C1869 (c) on 31 May 1917. The body was exhumed on 14 July 1917 by licence of the Home Secretary dated 3 July 1917 and re-interred on the same day in Section E6805B. The grave is not marked by a stone.
Brother of William Beer (9), nephew of Annie Beer (30) and cousin of Annie Beer (2), who were also killed in the raid. Son of Harry Beer, a coal porter and marine fireman. The bomb fell close to the Beer family, all of whom were immediately killed by the force of the blast.

BEER, William James
Age: 9
Address: 67 Bridge Street, Folkestone.
Died in Tontine Street from a bad chest wound. Buried in Cheriton Road Cemetery Section C5788 (c) on 31 May 1917. The body was exhumed on 14 July 1917 by licence of the Home Secretary dated 3 July 1917 and re-interred on the same day in Section E6805B. A gravestone was not found.
Brother of Arthur Beer (11) and nephew of Annie Beer (30) and cousin of Annie Beer (2), who were also killed in the raid. Son of Harry Beer, a coal porter and marine fireman, Willie and his brother were staying with their aunt while their father was at work. It is said the two boys were kicking a ball to each other to relieve the boredom of standing in the queue.

BLOODWORTH, George Henry
Age: 19
Address: serving soldier at Shorncliffe Army Camp.
Fatally injured in Bouverie Road East in the head and heart, died the same day at West Cliff Hospital. Buried at Shorncliffe Military Cemetery Grave No.O.555 on 29 May 1917. The gravestone is in excellent condition. George was born at Lee and was the son of George and Mary Bloodworth of 18 Banstead Street, Nunhead. He was originally Private G/78071 in the 29th Battalion, Middlesex Regiment before being transferred to the 5th Battalion, Labour Corps. He was walking in company with Kathleen Chapman when shrapnel from an exploding bomb mortally wounded both of them.

BLOODWORTH, George Henry

BOWBRICK, Gertrude Elizabeth
Age: 12

Address: 81 Ashley Avenue, Cheriton. Died in Tontine Street. Burial place not traced. Gertrude was killed along with her younger sister Mabel. Their mother, Nellie, was seriously injured and spent the remainder of her life in the Royal Victoria Hospital until her death on 24 March 1925.

BOWBRICK, Gertrude Elizabeth

Gertie was a bright and attractive girl with a real zest for life.

BOWBRICK, Mabel Esther
Age: 9

Address: 81 Ashley Avenue, Cheriton. Died in Tontine Street. Burial place not traced. Mabel was out shopping with her mother and elder sister Gertrude when the bomb fell on Tontine Street. The two sisters were killed immediately and their mother was seriously injured. The father of the girls was Walter Bowbrick, a builder's foreman.

BOWBRICK, Mabel Esther

BROCKWAY, Sydney
Age: 63

Address: 17 Peter Street, Folkestone. Died in Tontine Street from injuries to the back of the head. Buried in Cheriton Road Cemetery Section C1855 (c) on 30 May 1917. The gravestone remains in fair condition.

Sydney worked for Folkestone Corporation as a labourer. He was born in Wiltshire and was married to Sarah (born in Gloucester) who was 59 at the time of her husband's death. They had six children – Emma (b.1885), Frederick (b.1887), Alice (b.1889), Charles (b.1892), William (b.1894) and Edith (b.1896).

BURGIN, Dorothy Lilian
Age: 16

Address: 21 Oaks Road, Cheriton. Fatally injured in Oaks Road, died that same evening in the Royal Victoria Hospital. Burial place not traced. Dorothy worked as a laundress in Cheriton. She was standing in front of her house with her sister Rose and friend Mabel Ellender when the bombs began to fall. Badly frightened, the three girls ran towards a footbridge a hundred yards distant, but were hit by shrapnel from a bomb. Dorothy was the worst hit and was carried home by a police constable before being taken to hospital.

BURKE, David John ('John')
Age: 42

Address: 29 St Winifred Road, Folkestone. Died in Bouverie Road East from a deep gash in the right temple. Buried in Cheriton Road Cemetery Section C340 (u) on 1 June 1917. The gravestone remains in good condition. Mr Burke was a boot- and shoe-repairer at 21 Bouverie Road East. He was killed when a bomb exploded outside his shop and threw him across the road against the railings of the County School for Girls. Some reports say his head was severed from his body.

BURVILL, Hilda Elizabeth
Age: 20

Address: Hope Cottage, Black Bull Road, Folkestone. Fatally injured in the legs and body in Tontine Street, died in the West Cliff Hospital on 26 May 1917. Buried in Cheriton Road Cemetery Section C1856 (c) on 30 May 1917. The inscription on the gravestone is now faded. Hilda's father, Albert Burvill, was a well-known figure in the town because of his employment by the Radnor Estate as a policeman to ensure the select Leas and West End of the town remained free of 'undesirables'. By 1901, Albert (b. 1863) and his wife Margaret (b.1860) had had six children Mabel (b.1887), Albert (b.1889), Henry (b.1891), Stephen (b.1893), Hilda (b.1897) and Mary (b.1900). A relative of Hilda's, Jimmy Burvill, was killed in the Second World War when his pub, the Wheatsheaf, was flattened by a doodlebug that hit Bridge Street on 3 July 1944.

BURVILL, Hilda Elizabeth

BUTCHER, George Edward
Age: 44
Address: 27 Alexandra Street, Folkestone.
Fatally injured in Foord Road, died in the Royal Victoria Hospital on 5 June 1917. Buried in Cheriton Road Cemetery Section B68 (u) on 8 June 1917. The gravestone remains in good condition. George, who was born in Wye, had been employed as a coal carter for Scrivener's for 23 years and was on his rounds during that fateful Friday evening. He had just left his horse and cart to speak to an acquaintance named Charles Savage when a bomb fell behind the hoardings at the junction of Foord, Black Bull and Radnor Park roads, which severely wounded him behind the left knee. He was taken to the Royal Victoria Hospital, where his left leg was amputated, but he died on 5 June of toxaemia. His widow, Edith, who came from Folkestone and was four years younger than George, was eventually buried with him.

CASON, Annie Elizabeth
Age: 46
Address: 24 Royal Military Avenue, Cheriton.
Died in Tontine Street from wounds to the face and neck. Burial place not traced. Wife of Arthur Charles Cason, Barrack Warden at Shorncliffe Army Camp. Annie had gone to Gosnold's to buy a new dress and was found dead in the shop from severe blast injuries.

CASTLE, Albert Edward

CASTLE, Albert Edward
Age: 41
Address: 27 Wear Bay Crescent, Folkestone.
Died in the grounds of Grange School, Shorncliffe Road when the main artery in his neck was cut by shrapnel (another report says it was a piece of guttering). Buried in Cheriton Road Cemetery Section C1866 (c) on 1 June 1917. The grave is not marked by a stone. Albert was a retired naval man who worked as a gardener at the Grange School. The pleasant spring sunshine had enticed Albert to spend a little longer tending the grounds at

CHAPMAN,
Kathleen

the school, which lay close to the main railway line. He had been having a laugh and joke with a couple of girl pupils just a few minutes before the bombs began to fall.

CHAPMAN, Kathleen
Age: 16
A native of Chilham Lees, Kent, she was employed as a chambermaid at the Bates Hotel, Sandgate Road. Fatally injured in Bouverie Road East, died in the Royal Victoria Hospital on 29 May 1917 from chest and head wounds. Burial place not traced.
Daughter of Alfred Chapman, Kathleen was walking in company with George Bloodworth on her way to collect a pair of shoes from John Burke's shop at 21 Bouverie Road East, when they were mortally wounded by shrapnel. She was described by the hotel's manager as a cheerful and conscientious girl who was popular with the hotel's guests.

CLARK, William (Willie)
Age: 12
Address: 24 Mead Road, Folkestone.
Fatally injured in the legs in Tontine Street, died in Shorncliffe Military Hospital on 28 May 1917. Buried in Cheriton Road Cemetery Section C1873 (c) on 31 May 1917. The inscription on the gravestone is now faded. A cheeky and cheerful chap, Willie was the life and soul of his family and a keen Boy Scout. Two elder brothers were away serving at the Front. At 5.30 during the evening of the raid, he had taken his father's tea to his place of work at Tolputt's timber yard, Tram Road. Willie stayed with his dad until 6.00 and then hung around by the harbour before making his way up Tontine Street on his way home as the bomb fell. Despite the severe injuries to his legs, Willie hung on to life for three days after the raid.

CONSIDINE, Francis Henry
Age: 5
Address: lodging at 27 Oaks Road, Cheriton.
Fatally injured in the head in Oaks Road, died in Shorncliffe Military Hospital the same day from shock. Buried in Shorncliffe Military Cemetery. His gravestone remains in excellent condition. The boy's father, Corporal M Considine, was serving in the Canadian Army, and upon returning home soon after the raid had finished found his wife Christina had been hurt and his son Francis seriously injured on his bed. They had been wounded, along with two children and a man, by a bomb dropped in Oaks Road, thirty yards distant. Francis proved to be the worst sufferer, sustaining a bad head wound, and had to be carried by a police constable to his lodgings, while the others walked. Another bomb fell close to the party as they returned home, but there were no further injuries.

CONSIDINE,
Francis Henry

COOPER, Phyllis Aimes
Age: 9
Address: 3 Warwick Terrace, Morrison Road, Folkestone.
Fatally injured in the body in Tontine Street, died in the Royal Victoria

Royal Victoria Hospital

Hospital on 26 May 1917. Buried in Cheriton Road Cemetery Section A2765 (u) on 30 May 1917. A gravestone was not found.
Daughter of W W Cooper, a butcher's assistant, Phyllis was with her mum, who was injured. She was fearfully maimed by the bomb and was picked up from the road by Mr Reich, the jeweller, whose wife then carried Phyllis into Timothy Whites. The chemist, W B Metcalfe, attended to her before she was transferred to hospital, but Phyllis died the next day.

DANIELS, Albert Dennis
Age: 12
Address: Coombe Farm, Hawkinge
Died in Tontine Street from bad injuries to the chest.
Burial place not traced. Albert's father of the same name was a farmer, and the distinctive farmhouse still survives on the Alkham Valley Road. He was the nephew of Nellie Feist, and the cousin of Stanley Feist, who were killed with him in their cart, which still remained attached to their dead horse. They had gone shopping in Folkestone and just happened to be passing up Tontine Street on their way

home when the bomb fell.

DAY, Frederick Charles
Age: 47
Address: 3 Linden Crescent, Folkestone.
Died in Tontine Street from heart failure. Buried in Cheriton Road Cemetery Section C335 (u) on 30 May 1917. The site is not marked by a gravestone. A grocer's assistant, Frederick suffered from heart trouble and was a somewhat nervy individual. Upon hearing the explosion he went out into the street and then staggered back into the shop after suffering an apparent heart attack. He died a few minutes later.

DICKER, Edith Agnes
Age: 13
Address: 13 Richmond Street, Folkestone.
Died in Tontine Street, Edith's body was taken to the Royal Victoria Hospital. Buried in Cheriton Road Cemetery Section A1702 (c) with her mother on 30 May 1917. Daughter of Sarah Jane Dicker, who was also killed, and George Wilkie Dicker, manager of the Maypole Dairy. Judging by her photograph Edith was a very well-turned-out young lady.

DICKER, Edith Agnes

DICKER, Sarah Jane
Age: 41
Address: 13 Richmond Street, Folkestone.
Died in Tontine Street from injuries to many parts of the body, the deceased was taken to the Royal Victoria Hospital. Buried in Cheriton Road Cemetery Section A1702 (c) with her

DICKER,
Sarah Jane

daughter on 30 May 1917. The grave is marked by a tall column stone engraved with ivy. It is in fairly good condition though the top appears to have broken off. The elegant Mrs Dicker was wife of George Wilkie Dicker, manager of the Maypole Dairy, and mother of Edith Agnes Dicker, her only child, who was killed with her. It is believed they were shopping in Gosnold's when the bomb fell.

DOWN, Alfred Durrett
Age: 54
Address: 52 Royal Military Avenue, Cheriton.
Fatally injured at his home from a shrapnel wound in the side of the body, he was removed to hospital but never recovered consciousness.
Burial place not traced. A painter by trade, Alfred was working in his back garden when a bomb fell right beside him. He was born in Sandgate and married Catherine, of the same age, who came from Newington. By 1901 they had produced six children – Alfred (b. 1890), Thomas (b. 1891), George (b. 1893), Ada (b. 1896), John (b. 1898) and Rose (b. 1899) – all born in Cheriton.

DUKES, Florence Edith
Age: 18
Address: 3 Devonshire Place, Horn Street, Cheriton.
Died in Tontine Street. Buried in St Martin's Church, Cheriton with her mother, Florence Elizabeth Dukes, who was also killed in the raid. Their gravestone is in good condition and is also inscribed with the name of Harry Dukes (the husband and father), who

died on 26 March 1947, aged 80, and was interred in Norwood Cemetery. Florence was the daughter of Henry Barfert Dukes, a mercantile clerk, and Florence Elizabeth Dukes. She was employed as a housemaid and, being at home on holiday, had gone shopping with her mother.

DUKES, Florence Elizabeth
Age: 51
Address: 3 Devonshire Place, Horn Street, Cheriton.
Died in Tontine Street from injuries to the head and legs. Buried in St Martin's Church, Cheriton with her daughter Florence Edith Dukes, who was also killed in the raid.
The wife of Henry Barfert Dukes and mother of Florence Edith Dukes, who died with her.

EALES, Edith May
Age: 17
Address: 27 Dudley Road, Folkestone.
Fatally injured in both legs in Stokes's shop, Tontine Street, died in the Royal Victoria Hospital on 26 May 1917. Buried in Cheriton Road Cemetery Section C1863 (c) on 1 June 1917. When viewed in 1996, her gravestone was in a poor condition with the inscription barely legible. By September 2002 the stone had disappeared. Daughter of Arthur Eales, a marine porter, Edith was employed as a bookkeeper in Stokes's shop and was inside the building when it collapsed as a result of the bomb falling amongst the queue outside. She was due to have celebrated her 18th birthday on 27 May 1917.

EALES, Edith May

FEIST, Nellie
Age: 50
Address: Coombe Farm, Hawkinge.
Died in Tontine Street from injuries to the head and legs. Buried in the churchyard of the redundant St Michael the Archangel, Hawkinge, a haven of serenity just up the hill from the busy A20 trunk road. The grave also contains the remains of her grandson Stanley, who was killed with her in the raid, and her son Arthur Gordon Feist (26), who died in France on 17 July 1917. The gravestone is in a good condition.

Nellie was born in Shillingstone, Surrey in 1866 and married Arthur Feist (b.1863), a draper from Folkestone. Their first son, John James Stanley, was born in 1890, and their second, Arthur, a year later. She was lodging at Coombe Farm with her relatives during the First World War and on 25 May 1917 had gone into Folkestone in the horse and cart with her grandson Stanley and nephew Albert Daniels. They were passing up Tontine Street when the bomb fell and were all found dead in the cart.

FEIST, Stanley Albert (Sonny)
Age: 5
Address: Coombe Farm, Hawkinge.
Died in Tontine Street from injuries to the head and chest. Buried in the churchyard of St Michael the Archangel, Hawkinge with his grandmother Nellie, who was also killed in the raid, and his uncle, Arthur Gordon Feist (26), who was killed in France on 17 July 1917. The gravestone is in a good condition.

Sonny Feist was born on 11 December 1911 in Ashford to John Stanley and Edith Feist (née Bridges). His mother had been born at the New Inn, Elham in 1888 and after her marriage to

Stanley they had lived at 47 Linden Road, Ashford. Tragically Edith died at home on 12 April 1912 aged 23 from a severe nose bleed (possibly haemorrhaged). Stanley was then looked after by Nellie and was baptized at St Michael the Archangel, Hawkinge on 23 March 1913. He was

FEIST, Stanley Albert (Sonny)

on a shopping trip to Folkestone with Nellie and his cousin Albert Daniels when the raid on Folkestone commenced. The grave of Stanley's mother is in Cheriton Road Cemetery.

FRANCIS, Florence (Florrie)
Age: 33
Address: 46 Foord Road, Folkestone.

FRANCIS, Florence (Florrie)

Died in Tontine Street from bad injuries to the body, taken to the Royal Victoria Hospital. Buried in Cheriton Road Cemetery Section B386 (u) on 1 June 1917. The inscription is badly faded on her gravestone. Daughter of George and Rhoda Francis, Florrie was shopping with her friend Rose Hughes when the bomb fell. She is buried next to Rose and has a similar-styled gravestone.

GOULD, Edward Stephen
Age: 39
Address: Pavilion Stables, Tram Road, Folkestone.
Fatally injured in the body and legs in Tontine Street, died in the Royal

Victoria Hospital the same night. Buried in Cheriton Road Cemetery Section C1871 (c) on 1 June 1917. No gravestone is extant. A stableman, he was in company with his work colleague Richard Graves when the bomb exploded in Tontine Street.

GRAVES, Richard Ashby
Age: 40
Address: Pavilion Stables, Tram Road, Folkestone.

Fatally injured in the legs in Tontine Street, died in the Royal Victoria Hospital the same night. Buried in Cheriton Road Cemetery Section C1854 (c) on 29 May 1917. The inscription on the gravestone is becoming faint. A stableman at the Pavilion Stables, Dick Graves was walking in Tontine Street with his work colleague Edward Gould when the bomb fell. His son, who shared the same name, was added to Dick's grave after his death on 28 May 1919 aged 8.

GRAVES, Richard Ashby

GRIMES, Edith Mary (Edie)
Age: 24
Address: 14 Tontine Street, Folkestone. Died in Tontine Street from wounds to the head and body. Buried in Cheriton Road Cemetery Section C338 (u) on 30 May 1917. The gravestone remains in good condition. Born in Paris, Edie was employed by Messrs Atkinson and Stainer as a typist. She had a sister named Lily and a brother called Bertie, and was shopping with Bertie when the bomb fell. Flying shrapnel severely

GRIMES, Edith Mary (Edie)

wounded Edie in the head and though it is probable her death was almost instantaneous, she was taken to hospital and was officially pronounced dead some two hours later.

HALL, William Henry
Age: 64
Address: 68 Tontine Street, Folkestone. Fatally injured in the head in Tontine Street, died in the Royal Victoria Hospital on 27 May 1917. Buried in Cheriton Road Cemetery Section A1705 (c) on 1 June 1917. The gravestone remains in fairly good condition. A pork butcher, Mr Hall was fatally injured in his shop, which stood close to where the bomb fell.

He was born in Dover, as was his wife Isabelle, who was aged 62 at the time of her husband's death. Their daughter Charlotte was born in Folkestone in 1882.

HALL, William Henry

HAMBLY, Johanna Mary
Age: 67
Address: 32 Radnor Park Road, Folkestone. Died in Tontine Street when her head was severed. Buried in Cheriton Road Cemetery Section E7920 (c) on 31 May 1917. No gravestone was found. The widow of Captain Edgar Hambly, Johanna's head was never discovered.

HAMBROOK, Ethel L

HAMBROOK, Ethel L
Age: 12
Address: 1 Invicta Road, Folkestone. Died in Tontine Street from bad

injuries to the head and body. Buried in Cheriton Road Cemetery Section C1867 (c) on 31 May 1917. The inscription on the gravestone is becoming faded.

HARRIS, Caroline
Age: 35
Address: 144 Cheriton High Street, Cheriton.
Fatally injured in the legs and back in Tontine Street, was dead on arrival at the Royal Victoria Hospital. Buried in Cheriton Road Cemetery Section C1864 (c) on 1 June 1917. The inscription on the gravestone is beginning to fade. Caroline was the fifth of ten children born to William James Tyler and Elizabeth Parker of Peter Street, Folkestone. She was betrothed to Joseph Harris, who during the war joined the Cycle Corps. Caroline's sister Polly married a man named Taylor who ran a sweet shop in Denmark Street, Folkestone.

HARRISON, Fanny
Age: 39
Address: 15 Bournemouth Road, Folkestone.
Died in Tontine Street from bad wounds to the head and legs. Buried in Cheriton Road Cemetery Section C339 (u) on 30 May 1917. The headstone is in poor condition with the inscription badly faded. Fanny was a spinster of no occupation.

HAYES, Dennis William
HAYES, William Age: 2
Address: 25 East Street, Folkestone.
Died in Tontine Street from bad injuries all over his body. Buried in Cheriton Road Cemetery Section C5790 (c) on 31 May 1917.

No gravestone appears to be extant. The son of Martha Godden Hayes, who was also killed in the raid, Dennis was in the queue with his mum outside Stokes Bros when the bomb fell among them. It is sad to report that very little remained of him after the blast.

HAYES, Martha Godden
Age: 30
Address: 25 East Street, Folkestone.
Died in Tontine Street from bad injuries to the body. Buried in Cheriton Road Cemetery Section F8504 (c) on 30 May 1917. No gravestone was found. It is believed Martha was in the queue

HAYES, Martha Godden

outside Stokes's shop with her young son Dennis when the bomb fell among the shoppers. Her husband had been killed at the Front the previous year. Martha came from an old Folkestone fishing family and lived in a small street in the fishing quarter, close to the harbour.

HAYWARD, Louisa Alice
Age: 37
Address: 38 Thanet Gardens, Folkestone.
Died in Tontine Street from head injuries. Buried in Cheriton Road Cemetery Section A2758 (u) on 2 June 1917. No gravestone was found. Louisa was originally going to shop in the High Street that fateful evening, but changed her mind and went to Tontine Street instead. She was in Gosnold's when the bomb fell, and her body was so badly injured she had to be identified by her clothes and boots. (Another report says her body was blown over the back of Stokes's shop.) Louisa left four young children.

Her husband, William, was well-known in the town as the 'Newington Hero'. This was because at the age of ten he rescued his younger brother and sister from their wrecked home near Danton Pinch Farm, which had been crushed by a landslip of snow on 21 January 1891. William's parents and another sister were killed by the fall; and for his bravery he was awarded the Silver Medal of Honour by the Society of the Golden Cord. A tailor by trade, he was serving at the Front when this second great tragedy of his life occurred.

HICKMAN, Arthur David
Age: 6 (5 is sometimes quoted)

HICKMAN, Arthur David

Address: 93 Royal Military Avenue, Cheriton. Died in Tontine Street when his head was completely smashed. Burial place not traced (not listed in Shorncliffe Cemetery records). Arthur's father was a Sergeant Major in the Royal Scots, though for this photograph he was dressed in the then fashionable young boy's outfit of a white naval suit.

HOLLOWAY, Mary Philhemina
Age: 9
Address: 13 Burrow Road, Folkestone. Died in Tontine Street from smashed legs. Buried in Cheriton Road Cemetery Section C1067 (u) on 30 May 1917. The cross has been broken off the headstone, but the inscription is still visible. Mary's father Frederick Sidney Holloway was a bank clerk. She was with her mother (who was

HOLLOWAY, Mary Philhemina

injured) and her sister Veronica (who was killed) when the bomb fell on Tontine Street. Mary would have been ten in June 1917.

HOLLOWAY, Veronica Mary
Age: 16 months
Address: 13 Burrow Road, Folkestone. Fatally injured in the head and chest in Tontine Street, died in the Royal Victoria Hospital the same night.

HOLLOWAY, Veronica Mary

Buried in Cheriton Road Cemetery Section C1068 (u) on 30 May 1917. Veronica was laid to rest next to her sister Mary and both graves were marked with identical cross headstones. However, unlike Mary's, Veronica's cross remains intact and in quite good condition. Veronica was killed, along with her elder sister Mary, and their mother was seriously injured. However, Mrs Holloway recovered and continued to live at Burrow Road until the Second World War.

HORN, Edward James
Age: 45
Address: 8 Radnor Cliff, Sandgate. Died in the approach road to Folkestone Central railway station, off Cheriton Road, when his head was severed from his body. Buried at Waltham Church, his gravestone is in excellent condition. On the death of his widow Ellen in 1966, a new headstone was placed on the grave where Edward, Ellen and their eldest son Edward, who died in 1939 aged 37, lay. Their final resting place stands by the boundary wall of the church in

a very peaceful spot. Waltham is an isolated village, near to Canterbury, standing amongst some of the most beautiful countryside in Kent. Edward Horn was butler to Sir Thomas Devitt, of Radnor Cliff. At the time of his death he had gone to meet his employer, who was travelling down from London for the weekend, and had parked the carriage, with two horses, in the down-side approach road. Startled by the explosions, the horses had attempted to run away, and Mr Horn was endeavouring to stop them when a bomb fell close by, immediately killing both him and the horses. Originally hailing from Shalmsford Street, near Chartham, Edward later moved to Waltham. He left a widow, Ellen, and three sons.

HOUDARD, Constante
Age: 33
Address: 99 Linden Crescent, Folkestone.
Died in Tontine Street from a large wound in the chest, along with many other injuries. Buried in Shorncliffe Military Cemetery in the communal Belgian grave. Constante was a Belgian soldier, who was spending a rest period in Folkestone visiting relatives that had fled from the Germans at the beginning of the war. He was queuing for potatoes outside Stokes Bros with another Belgian soldier, Hyppolite Verschueren.

HUGHES, Rosina Caroline (Rose)
Age: 34
Address: 46 Foord Road, Folkestone.
Died in Tontine Street from

HUGHES, Rosina Caroline (Rose)

bad wounds to the body and legs. Buried in Cheriton Road Cemetery Section B409 (u) on 1 June 1917. The gravestone is in fairly poor condition. Rose, a schoolteacher, was the daughter of Joseph and Caroline Hughes of Northfleet, Kent. She was in company with her good friend Florrie Francis when they were both killed by the bomb that fell on Tontine Street. They were buried next to each other with very similar headstones.

JACKMAN, Dorothy Bertha
Age: 14
Address: 12 Connaught Road, Folkestone.
Died in Tontine Street from a large wound in the throat. Buried in Cheriton Road Cemetery Section C1859 (c) on 31 May 1917. No gravestone is extant.
Daughter of James Jackman,

JACKMAN, Dorothy Bertha

an electrician, Dorothy was killed along with her friends Gwennie Terry and Madge McDonald, who were lodging with her. They had gone to Tontine Street to have a look around the shops and were laughing and joking together outside Gosnold's when the bomb fell. Dorothy was killed instantly by a large piece of shrapnel that ripped into her throat.

LAXTON, Katherine Euphemia
Age: 72
Address: 19 East Cliff Gardens, Folkestone.
Died in Tontine Street when her legs were almost severed. Buried in Cheriton Road Cemetery Section A475 (c) on 29 May 1917. No gravestone was found. A widow, Katherine was standing amongst the queue outside the greengrocer's shop.

LEE, William
Age:
Address: 3 Marshland Road, New Eltham.
Died in Tontine Street. Burial place not traced. William Lee was in Folkestone on business making arrangements to take his donkeys to Dymchurch Sands for the summer season. His occupation was described as a 'general dealer'.

LYTH, Daniel Stringer
Age: 54 (born 10 September 1862)
Fatally injured in the legs by shrapnel at St Leonard's Church, Hythe, he was

LYTH, Daniel Stringer

taken to the Royal Victoria Hospital and operated on, but died during the night. Buried at Saltwood Church. His only son Daniel, who was killed in action in France on 19 April 1917, was laid to rest with him. The gravestone remains in good condition. Mr Lyth was Verger of Hythe Parish Church and a former Town Sergeant. He was killed by a bomb splinter that ripped into his right thigh while standing at the west door of the church. He had been engaged in conversation with the Vicar, Revd H D Dale, and his wife inside the church when they heard the explosions. As they went outside to investigate, a bomb fell in the churchyard shattering tombstones and sending shrapnel in all directions. The Vicar was saved from injury by a tin of throat lozenges in his coat pocket that deflected a piece of shrapnel, though his wife was injured in the face. Mr Lyth was Hythe's Town Sergeant for many years, and took

part in the Burma war with the King's Royal Rifles, for which he proudly wore a medal. He had resided in the town for over 20 years; his wife being a native of Hythe, and was a man of good qualities that he hid behind a natural reserve. Mrs Lyth had also recently lost two brothers; F Cloke at the Front and Herbert Cloke, who died suddenly at Hythe. She is said to have received £200 from the proprietors of the *Daily Mail*, having filled in a coupon. The paper revealed that a number of Folkestone sufferers also received cheques. After the war Mrs Lyth requested her husband's name be placed on Hythe's war memorial (unveiled in 1921) alongside her son for, although he had retired as a soldier, he was still a local volunteer.

McDONALD, Agnes Curran (Madge)
Age: 22
Address: lodging at 12 Connaught Road, Folkestone.
Fatally injured in Tontine Street, died in the Royal Victoria Hospital on 2 June 1917. Buried in Cheriton Road Cemetery Section C1874 (c) on 3 June 1917. A small simple stone bears her inscription. Madge McDonald was a Canadian typist who had come over to England to assist in war work. She was lodging with the Jackman family at 12 Connaught Road and was in Tontine Street with Dorothy Jackman and Gwennie Terry when the bomb fell. Madge was in Folkestone waiting to proceed to France to do ambulance work.

McDONALD, Albert Edward Charles (Charlie)

McDONALD, Albert Edward Charles (Charlie)
Age: 12
Address: 30 Stuart Road, Folkestone.

Died in Tontine Street from a bad wound in the chest. Buried in Cheriton Road Cemetery Section C1865 (c) on 1 June 1917. The gravestone remains in good condition. Son of Albert, a seaman, and Jessie McDonald, Charlie was an errand boy for Timothy Whites in Tontine Street and was out in the street when the bomb fell. His house backed onto the railway line at the Junction station and as a result Charlie became very fond of trains. He would spend hours looking out of his bedroom window and hoped to become a train driver when he was older.

MARSHMENT, Jane
Age: 50
Address: lodging at 21 Manor Road, Folkestone.
Died at 21 Manor Road when buried under the rubble of the house. Burial place not traced. A cook at the house, Jane's lifeless body, with the feet cut clean off, was not recovered for 24 hours owing to the amount of rubble to be cleared. The body was eventually taken to the cemetery mortuary on Saturday night. Jane had been trying to leave the building when she was overwhelmed by an avalanche of debris.

MAXTED, Elizabeth
Age: 31
Address: 5 Grove Road, Folkestone.

MAXTED, Elizabeth

Died in Tontine Street from severe wounds to the head and legs. Buried in Cheriton Road Cemetery Section A1700 (c) on 30 May 1917. The gravestone remains in good condition. Wife of William Arthur Maxted, a butcher's manager.

McGUIRE, Ernest Henry
Age: 6
Address: 15 Linden Crescent, Folkestone.
Died in Tontine Street from bad injuries to the head and body. Buried in Cheriton Road Cemetery Section C5764 (c) on 29 May 1917. The gravestone is in quite good condition, but is threatened by weeds during the

McGUIRE, Ernest Henry

summer as it lies close to the western boundary of the cemetery. Little Ernie was the son of Harry McGuire, fireman. His mother was injured in the raid.

MOSS, Jane Charlotte May
Age: 20
Address: 204 Cheriton High Street, Cheriton.
Died in Tontine Street from wounds in both legs. Burial place not traced (not listed in Shorncliffe Military Cemetery records). Wife of Private George Moss (Labour Battalion) and mother of Walter Moss, who was also killed. Private Moss came from Chatham, Ontario and enlisted at the beginning of the war in August 1914. He lost four brothers, his father-in-law and one cousin during the war, in addition to his wife and son. A member of the Salvation Army, he hoped to become a chaplain.

MOSS, Walter George
Age: 2
Address: 204 Cheriton High Street, Cheriton.

Corporal George Moss

Died in Tontine Street from a large hole in the chest. Burial place not traced (not listed in Shorncliffe Military Cemetery records). Son of Jane Moss, who was also killed, and Corporal George Moss, who was serving in the Labour Battalion. Walter was the first victim of the raid to be received at the Royal Victoria Hospital, but was dead on arrival.

NORRIS, Florence Kathleen

NORRIS, Florence Kathleen
Age: 2
Address: 30 Black Bull Road, Folkestone.
Died in Tontine Street when her head was severed. Buried in Cheriton Road Cemetery Section C5762 (c) on 30 May 1917 with her mother and brother. The body was exhumed on 14 July 1917 by licence of the Home Secretary dated 3 Jure-interred on the same day Section E6783A.The gravestone remains in good condition, but is buried beneath undergrowth on the southern boundary of the cemetery near the railway. Daughter of Florence and sister of William, who were also killed. It was probably little Florence's head that was discovered on the step of the Brewery Tap. A large bloodstain was said to have remained for many years, despite numerous attempts to clean it off.

NORRIS, Florence Louise
Age: 24
Address: 30 Black Bull Road, Folkestone.
Died in Tontine Street. Buried in Cheriton Road Cemetery Section C1851(c) on 30 May 1917 with her two children. The body was exhumed on 14 July 1917 by licence of the Home Secretary dated 3 July 1917 and re-interred on the same day in Section E6783A. Mother of Florence (2) and William (10 months), who were also killed. Her

NORRIS, Florence Louise

husband William Alfred, a motor mechanic, lost all three members of his family. The house where the Norris family lived is little altered today and, with its old, black front door, is perhaps still in mourning for its lost occupants.

NORRIS, William Alfred
Age: 10 months
Address: 30 Black Bull Road, Folkestone.
Died in Tontine Street from head and chest injuries. His body was taken to the Royal Victoria Hospital. Buried in Cheriton Road Cemetery Section C5762 (c) on 30 May 1917 with his mother and sister. The body was exhumed on 14 July 1917 by licence of the Home Secretary dated 3 July 1917 and re-interred on the same day in Section E6783A.
Son of Florence Louise (24) and brother of Florence Kathleen (2) who were killed with him. William's little body was found dead in his pram, which had been blown across the street.

NORRIS, Florence Louise, NORRIS, Florence Kathleen, NORRIS, William Alfred

PARKER, Amy Gertrude
Age: 42
Address: 50 Ormonde Road, Hythe.
Died in Ormonde Road, Hythe from shrapnel wounds. Burial place not traced. The widow of Mr Ernest Edward Parker, Mrs Parker was by profession a wardrobe dealer. Upon hearing the explosions she had gone out into the street to tell her child to

come indoors when she was hit by a piece of shrapnel that passed into her body through a shoulder and penetrated the heart, causing almost instant death.

REED, Mabel
Age: 12
Address: 32 Mead Road, Folkestone.
Fatally injured in Tontine Street, died in the Royal Victoria Hospital from injuries to the chest and legs that same night. Buried in Cheriton Road Cemetery Section C1857 (c) on 30 May 1917. The inscription on the gravestone is now very faded.
The daughter of Charles Reed, a cab driver, Mabel had been taken by her mother to buy a coat in Gosnold's and they had just left the shop when the bomb fell outside Stokes's shop. Mrs Reed was also injured and was taken by horse and cart to the Royal Victoria Hospital, where a doctor, after examining her, passed by, saying she would not live. Fortunately a Canadian doctor came along at the same time and disagreed. He took her to Shorncliffe Military Hospital for an operation, which left her unconscious for a month. Every day, soldiers sat by her bed looking for signs of life. Eventually she recovered sufficiently to go home, but was dogged forever afterwards with a bad leg, which had been injured by shrapnel.
Mabel's sister Annie had been given a halfpenny to stay at home and was playing outside with her brothers Jack and Fred when they heard a bang. A neighbour took the three children inside and they went to stay with a friend of their father when their mother and sister failed to return home. Years later, in 1930, the family were told by lawyers that the Germans had paid out compensation to the civilians injured during the raid, but the money never found its way to those concerned.

ROBINSON, John Walter Francis (Jackie)
Age: 5
Address: 64 St Michael's Street, Folkestone.
Died in Tontine Street from bad head and leg injuries. Buried in Cheriton Road Cemetery Section C5787 (c) on 1 June 1917. The gravestone is in quite good condition. Young Jackie was the son of Corporal John and Grace Robinson and was noted for his big mop of dark brown hair. He was out shopping with his mother when the bomb fell, and was killed instantly. Mrs Robinson was badly injured herself, but never got over the fact that she had survived while her darling Jackie had been taken away.

ROBINSON, John Walter Francis (Jackie)

RUMSEY, Florence (Florrie)
Age: 17
Address: 29 Black Bull Road, Folkestone.
Fatally injured in the head in Stokes's shop, Tontine Street, Florrie was initially taken to the Royal Victoria Hospital, but was transferred to Shorncliffe Military Hospital, where she died on 27 May 1917. Buried in Cheriton Road Cemetery Section C1862 (c) on 31 May 1917. Florrie's grave, which is in a good condition, lies under a tree, and until a recent tidy-up was engulfed by branches and twigs. Florrie was the daughter of George Rumsey, a fish merchant, and his wife Louisa. She was born in Folkestone in

RUMSEY, Florence (Florrie)

1900 at 7 Linden Crescent, as was her sister Emmeline, who was a year younger.
Florrie was employed as a bookkeeper in Stokes's shop and was inside the building when the bomb fell outside and sent it crashing down on the occupants. It was initially thought that Florrie might survive, but two days after the raid she succumbed to her horrific head injuries.

SNOAWERT, Marie
Age: 44
Address: 7 Copthall Gardens, Folkestone.
Fatally injured in Tontine Street, Marie eventually died of her injuries on 26 June 1917. Buried in Cheriton Road Cemetery Section C346 (c) on 30 June 1917. The site is not marked with a stone. The forgotten victim of the raid who was left off the official Folkestone death-toll (71) because she did not succumb to her injuries until a month after the raid. Marie was a nurse from Malines, Belgium who escaped to England after the death of her husband during the German invasion. She was lodged at 7 Copthall Gardens with other Belgian refugees and was out shopping in Tontine Street with two of them, Elizabeth Bosmans and Paul Merton (both injured), when the bomb fell.
After the raid she was admitted to the sanatorium on 7 June suffering from scarlet fever, wounds in the right thigh and extensive ecchymosis. She died 19 days later of 'phlebitis caused by wounds received during the air raid'.

SPARKES, Gladys Alice
Age: 18
Address: 15 Providence Place, Providence Street, South

Ashford, Ashford.
Killed in Providence Place by a bomb that exploded 40 feet in the air. Buried in Ashford Borough Cemetery on 28 May 1917. No gravestone was found. The first victim of the air raid, Gladys had gone out into the street upon hearing the explosions and was blown against a wall by the blast. She was the daughter of Charles Sparkes and had two sisters, Grace and Minnie, and a brother, Willie. Amongst the wreaths at her funeral was one from the underwear factory, where Gladys probably worked.

STOKES,
Arthur Ernest

STOKES, Arthur Ernest (wrongly described as William Edward in the newspapers)
Age: 14
Address: 33a Harvey Street, Folkestone.
Fatally injured in his father's shop in Tontine Street, died in Shorncliffe Military Hospital at 4.10 am on 28 May 1917 from shrapnel wounds to the legs. Buried in Cheriton Road Cemetery Section L3653 (u) on 1 June 1917 with his father. The gravestone remains in good condition.
Arthur was the son of William Stokes (also killed), the joint owner of Stokes's shop, which was devastated by the Tontine Street bomb. He was born on 23 April 1903 at 33a Harvey Street, Folkestone. Earlier in the day he had gone bluebell picking with a friend, but, being particularly enthusiastic about his father's business, he had gone to the shop to help out shortly before the bomb fell. Young Arthur's death greatly affected his family, who rued the hand of fate in sending him back to the shop.

STOKES, William Henry
Age: 46
Address: 33a Harvey Street, Folkestone. Fatally injured in his shop in Tontine Street, died during the same evening at the Royal Victoria Hospital from bad injuries to the back and legs. Buried in Cheriton Road Cemetery Section L3653 (u) on 1 June 1917 with his son Arthur, who was also killed in the raid. The gravestone remains in good condition. William was born at Bulwark Hill, Hougham on 28 October 1870, the eldest child of William Stokes and Mary Chapman. They were to have six sons altogether: William, George, Fred, Jack, Bob and Ben. William married Jane Dixon, eight years his senior, and they had six children. The brothers were all prominent local businessmen. William ran the Tontine Street shop with George, while Bob and Ben operated the branch at 47 Bouverie Road West. In addition William, George and Jack operated the Folkestone Shipping Company, importing coal on their lugger 'The Luz' to Folkestone, where it was kept in their store at Dover Road, run by Jack.

STOKES, William Henry

TERRY, Edith Gwendoline (Gwennie)
Age: 13
Address: 12 Connaught Road, Folkestone. Died in Tontine Street when one leg was blown off and the

TERRY, Edith Gwendoline (Gwennie)

other was left hanging by a thread. Buried in Cheriton Road Cemetery Section C1858 (c) on 31 May 1917. The grave has no headstone, but its sides are inscribed. Daughter of Mr J Terry, a railway official at Folkestone Central Station, Gwennie was in company with her friends Dorothy Jackman (who was also instantly killed) and Madge McDonald (who later died of her injuries) when the bomb fell in Tontine Street. Gwennie (as everyone knew her) was said to have been an exceptionally pretty girl with long blonde hair.

VANE, Alfred
Age: 35
Address: 8 Bradstone New Road, Folkestone.
Fatally injured in Tontine Street, died in Shorncliffe Military Hospital from shrapnel wounds to the head. Burial place not known. Alfred worked as a jobbing gardener. He was walking up Tontine Street, a little distance from where the bomb fell, when he was hit in the head by shrapnel.

VERSCHUEREN, Hyppolite
Age: 41
Address: Sandgate Road, Folkestone. Died in Tontine Street when his head was partially blown up and his body was badly punctured by shrapnel. Buried in Shorncliffe Military Cemetery in the communal Belgian grave. A Belgian soldier based at staff quarters, he was killed along with fellow national Constante Houdard.

WALTON, Doris Eileen Spencer
Age: 16
Address: The Mount, Julian Road, Folkestone, (where she was a school pupil). Fatally injured in the grounds

of Athelstan Ladies' School, Shorncliffe Road, whilst playing tennis when hit in the stomach by a bomb fragment. Doris succumbed to her injuries the next day at the Royal Victoria Hospital. Buried in Cheriton Road Cemetery Section A431 (c) on 29 May 1917. No gravestone was found. Doris lived at 25 Bernard Gardens, Wimbledon, but was a boarder at the Mount School, Julian Road. She was unluckily killed by a piece of shrapnel that fell in allotment gardens some 300 yards away. Her tennis partner was fortunate in not being hit, though her tennis racket was riddled with shrapnel.

WAUGH, Elizabeth Charlotte

WAUGH, Elizabeth Charlotte
Age: 48
Address: 26 North Street, Folkestone (given in error in the newspapers as 47 Dover Road).
Died in Tontine Street from injuries all over the body.
Buried in Cheriton Road Cemetery Section C1860 (c) on 31 May 1917, Elizabeth's resting place is not marked by a gravestone. Wife of John Waugh, a soldier on foreign service, Elizabeth was a needlewoman by trade. Her daughter Elizabeth Mary was aged 18 at the time of her mother's death.

WILSON, Isabel
Age: 80

WILSON, Isabel
Address: 11 East Street, Folkestone.
Died in Tontine Street when her face, arms and legs were badly injured.
Buried in Cheriton Road Cemetery Section F8687 (c) on 31 May 1917. No

gravestone was found. Mrs Wilson, the oldest victim of the raid, was the widow of James Wilson, a market-gardener. They had five children; Susan, Margaret, Ann, William and John. Isabel, whose maiden name was Skene, was born in the Borders area of Scotland, but came to live in the now-demolished old fishing quarter of Folkestone, in a narrow street tucked in behind The Stade. She was in the queue for potatoes outside Stokes's shop when the bomb fell. This photograph of Isabel is part of one taken to celebrate four generations of the family, as she had just become a great-grandmother.

List of injured

The named 102 civilians injured in the raid are listed below; however, there were certainly others that were not listed in the newspapers and official documents of the time (some sources put the total injured at 195). Three people – George Butcher, Agnes McDonald and Marie Snoawert – who were on the original list of Folkestone injured soon succumbed to their wounds and so are not included in this list.

Allen, Mrs – 14 Castle Hill Avenue, Folkestone
Anslow, Clara – 17 Fern Bank Crescent, Folkestone
Anslow, Frederick – 17 Fern Bank Crescent, Folkestone (child)
Ash, W T – 42 Pavilion Road, Folkestone
Attwood – Westbourne Gardens, Folkestone
Back, William – 28 Black Bull Road, Folkestone

Banks, Matilda – 11 Bouverie Square, Folkestone

Batchelor, John – 24 Radnor Park Crescent, Folkestone

Birkett, F – 5 Connaught Road, Folkestone

Bosmans, Elizabeth – 7 Copthall Gardens, Folkestone (Belgian)

Bowbrick, Lily Caroline (Nellie) – 81 Ashley Avenue, Cheriton (later, on 24 March 1925 succumbed to complications from her injuries received)

Brooke, Thomas – 36 Bridge Street, Ashford

Brooks, Leonard – 27 St John's Street, Folkestone (child)

Brooman, Horace – 33 Morehall Avenue, Folkestone

Brown, Miss – 9 Radnor Bridge Road, Folkestone

Burden, Ernest – 13 Providence Street, Ashford (child)

Burgin, Rose – 21 Oaks Road, Cheriton

Bury, Beatrice – 82 Linden Crescent, Folkestone

Cadwell, Eileen – 12 East Cliff Gardens, Folkestone

Caplin, Cissie – 41 Tontine Street, Folkestone

Challis, Mrs – 16 Ethelbert Road, Folkestone

Chantler, Grace – 24 Darlington Street, Folkestone (child)

Chittenden, Hilda – 28 St John's Street, Folkestone (child)

Clark, John – 26 St John's Street, Folkestone

Clark, Mrs – 16 East Street, Folkestone

Cloke, Sidney – 20 Linden Crescent, Folkestone

Coleman, Lily – 28 St John's Street, Folkestone

Collar, William – Red Cow Inn, Foord Road, Folkestone

Considine, Christina – 27 Oaks Road, Cheriton

Cooper, Mrs – 3 Warwick Terrace, Morrison Road, Folkestone

Croucher, Harry – 38 Garden Road, Folkestone

Dale, Mrs H D – The Parish Church Vicarage, Hythe

Davey, Ernest – 46 Royal Military Avenue, Cheriton

Drury, Beatrice – 82 Linden Crescent, Folkestone

Duff, Mrs – 43 Queen Street, Folkestone

Dunk, W – 92 Cheriton Road, Folkestone

Eadie, Jeannette – West Cliff Shades Inn, Connaught Road, Folkestone

Ellender, Mabel – 21 Oaks Road, Cheriton

Fagg, Dorothy – 17 Fern Bank Crescent, Folkestone

Featherbe, Kate – 68a Marshall Street, Folkestone

Flower, Maud – 3 Pavilion Road, Folkestone

Francis, Palmer – 1 Millfield, Folkestone

Friend, Edward – 8 Gloucester Place, Folkestone

Goldsmith, Miss – 60 Coolinge Road, Folkestone

Gosnold, George – 69 Tontine Street, Folkestone

Harvey, Mrs – 93 Dover Road, Folkestone

Hayes, Peter – 5 Black Bull Road, Folkestone

Higgins, Albert – 49 Tontine Street, Folkestone

Hoad, Alfred – 10 Ethelbert Road, Folkestone

Holloway, Alice – 13 Burrow Road, Folkestone

Hook, James – 26 Providence Street, Ashford

Houlden, Walter – 72 Tontine Street, Folkestone

Hunt, Henry – 35 Royal Military Avenue, Cheriton

Iden, Annie – 39 Greenfield Road, Folkestone

Jaion, Mrs – 102 Radnor Park Road, Folkestone

Jenner, Annie – 21 Manor Road, Folkestone

Jenner, C

Jones, John – 9 Radnor Bridge Road, Folkestone

Jones, Miss S – 10 Dover Road, Folkestone

Jordan, Mary – 56 Tontine Street, Folkestone

Larkin, Lily – 9 Thanet Gardens, Folkestone (child)

Leadbrates, Margaret – 59 Bournemouth Road, Folkestone

Long, Mrs – 46 Royal Military Avenue, Cheriton

McGuire, Mrs – 15 Linden Crescent, Folkestone

Marsh, Beryl – 29 Castle Hill Avenue, Folkestone

Matthews, John – 12 Alma Road, Cheriton

Merton, Paul – 7 Copthall Gardens (Belgian child)

Miller, James – 3 Garden Road, Folkestone

Milton, Lily – 6 South Street, Folkestone

Moererams D'Emanus – (Belgian)

Moore, Adelaide

Morris, J

Moyes, J

Muir, A J

Murphy, Mary Ann – 6 Grimston Gardens, Folkestone

Nash, Edward – 63 Dudley Road, Folkestone

Nicholls, Emily – 12 Albert Road, Hythe

Nicholls, Jane – 12 Albert Road, Hythe

Osborn, Miss – 3 East Cliff Villas, Folkestone

Palmer, G

Patrick, Daisy – 107 Canterbury Road, Folkestone

Payne, Bessie – 13 Bond Road, Folkestone

Miss Pegden

Ramsey, G – 44 Grimston Gardens, Folkestone

Reed, Mrs – 32 Mead Road, Folkestone

Reich, Francis J – 74 Tontine Street, Folkestone

Robinson, Mrs – 64 St Michael's Street, Folkestone

Savage, Charles V – 31 Shellons Street, Folkestone

Scrivens, John – 19 Watkin Road, Folkestone

Shelver, Florence – 62 Black Bull Road, Folkestone

Sherran, Mrs – 5 Harvey Street, Folkestone

Smith, Sarah – 16 Palmerston Street, Folkestone

Springate, Winnie – 66 Tontine Street, Folkestone

Stokes, Frederick C – 12 St John's Church Road, Folkestone (later died of his injuries on 11 October 1918)

Ticehurst, Matilda – 52 Black Bull Road, Folkestone

Thompson, S – 8 Grimston Gardens, Folkestone

Thorn, Mary – 49 St Michael's Street, Folkestone

Vandenbroele, Eugene – 39 Cheriton Road, Folkestone (Belgian)

Vane, Mrs – 45 Wear Bay Crescent, Folkestone

Waite, John – 51 Tontine Street, Folkestone

Whiting, George – 15 Great Fenchurch Street, Folkestone

Whiting, Rose – 70 Marshall Street, Folkestone

Wilson, Mrs – Wesleyan Soldiers'

Home, West Sandling, near Hythe

Frederick Charles Stokes was the only one of the six Stokes brothers not involved in the family business. He was a telegrapher; one of only seven such trained to transmit information from war zones and a keen member of Folkestone Rowing Club. He was born at Charlton, Dover and married Albina Warner from Sturry on 31 December 1899. They had five children, but sadly Albina passed away on 27 October 1906. Frederick married for a second time in March 1909 and fathered another son in November 1909. He never got over the injuries he received in the raid and eventually died at his home on 11 October 1918 from phthisis and pulmonary haemorrhage.

A family picture of the Stokes family in 1907. Left to right back row: Jack, George, William (killed in the raid), Fred (severely injured in the raid). Left to right front row: Mary, Ben William Snr, Bob. Mrs Howard

Newly dug graves in Cheriton Road Cemetery, Folkestone. Marlinova Collection

The burials of Sarah and Edith Dicker in Cheriton Road Cemetery on 30 May 1917.
Marlinova Collection

Three young girls pay their respects to a friend. The funeral expenses of Folkestone residents killed in the raid, which amounted to just over £316, were paid for by the Corporation.
Marlinova Collection

The funeral of a Folkestone air-raid victim in Cheriton Road Cemetery. Peter and Annie Bamford

Chapter Eight

SHRAPNEL ON THE TEA TABLE

PERSONAL REMINISCENCES OF THE 25 MAY 1917 RAID

Mrs Wyn Knowles recalled in the book *The Last Voices of St Mary's*:

One of my first memories is of the bombing in Tontine Street. I remember coming up the steps of my house and standing there to watch a line of buses coming along with lots of wounded people laid on the seats. They were taken to the hospital (the Royal Victoria) around the corner from us. I also remember seeing a man running along towards the hospital with a baby in his arms, and the baby was covered in blood.

Edith Vye remembered in the book *The Last Voices of St Mary's*:

When I was little, during the First World War, one day I was walking in Tontine Street with two friends of mine, two little girls, and suddenly the planes came over and a man grabbed me by the arm and pulled me in the Clarendon pub [Edith may have meant the Brewery Tap; the Clarendon was at the other end of the street] *and just then the bomb fell and my two friends were killed. There were babies in prams outside the shops and some of them had their heads blown off. It was an awful sight, a carnage, there were horses lying in the street cut to pieces. I was so shaken I didn't know what to do. Eventually I ran home and I was sobbing all the way.*

Mrs Florence Green (née Ramell) in a letter sent to her sister in America (who was a survivor of the *Titanic* disaster):

We are all well after the raid. You will have received a newspaper with a list of those killed and injured.

I happened to be having my tea at the shop when the whole affair happened. I heard the engines coming and, being different to the noise made by our aeroplanes, I began to feel uncomfortable, and just then a bomb exploded at the back of us.

Practically every glass in St John's Street was broken. All the staff, including myself rushed out to the front. I saw everything going into the air down Tontine Street. You know how terrible it is thinking every minute is going to be one's last.

It was the awful sights I witnessed after the actual raid that made me feel queer. Everyone from Tontine Street was brought past the shop [Thomas Ramell, family coachbuilders, 23 Dover Road] *and when I tell you it was a real slaughterhouse, you can guess how many were taken from there alone – quite 60, and heaps of soldiers were killed also.*

The plate glass window was broken at the shop, and nearly everything fell down in the affair. Sixty bombs were rained on us and damage was also done in Manor Road, Bouverie Road East and around the Central Station.

Bombs were dropped all down the line and also near home, so you will see how narrowly we escaped. What is to be will be, but my only desire is that they never come here anymore. If that is an air raid, well I never want to see another. We have a siren now, and on the approach of hostile aircraft that thing is sounded, and it's quite some noise!

Edith Cole, who was living at the time in Bradstone Avenue:

I recall seeing the planes through my bedroom window. It was about five o'clock [it must have been about an hour later] *on a sunny afternoon and they looked beautiful with the sun on their wings.*

But they did terrible damage when they dropped their bombs. People were gathering up anything they could find to take the injured to hospital. There were wounded people piled on carts, and others running up to the Victoria Hospital with children in their arms.

The planes came across the Foord Road Viaduct and then there was a roar of explosions. The news spread very quickly. One person told the next and soon the streets were filled with people looking for their relatives because Tontine Street was a major shopping street in those days.

There were tiny pieces of shrapnel both in the garden and my bedroom and I suppose I had a lucky escape too in a way. A little while before the bombs fell I suggested to my mother that we should go shopping, but she said I would have to wait until Dad came home.

Mrs Gold:

The aeroplanes over Folkestone looked like doves flying up in the clouds. When I got to Tontine Street men were putting the dead on a brewer's dray. Later on, when everything was peaceful, only Red Cross nurses and ambulances could be seen, except that there were queues outside the hospital of people trying to find or recognise their lost ones, it was like Earth turned to Heaven, the angels being the nurses.

On the Sunday a service was held in Radnor Park for the dead – another agonising sight, just one big patch of mourning. I had lost several friends; yet my husband (that is now), my brother, and several cousins went all through the war without a wound.

_____ _____ Tontine Street:

On the evening of 25th May 1917, living in Folkestone then, I was playing cricket with my young cousin in the park, when, without warning, the heavens seemed to collapse. To make a bolt for home was my first thought, but I had no sooner taken the first step than some premonition forced me flat on the ground: I tugged my cousin with me. At the same time a bomb exploded not twenty yards in front of us.

Tearing for home again, we heard that our place was on fire. Terror gripped me as I ran on. At last we came to our street, Tontine Street, and I shall never forget that scene. Squeezing my way through a barrier, I ran as if for my life as I saw my home, our business home, practically in ruins. Mother was in a state of collapse, and father had shrapnel in his lung.

Customers in the shop had been decapitated. Others were wounded beyond recognition, and they lay everywhere. There was a terrible amount of blood about. Two horses lay dead, shockingly mangled, and a 50ft gas flame from a penetrated main added to the horror.

Upstairs in the living rooms everything was chaos. I saw fragments of bodies, which had to be collected for identification purposes. It was more like a slaughterhouse than a home.

Hon A E Gathorn-Hardy, staying in Folkestone:

After tea, a little before 6, I went out to smoke a pipe on the Front. I sat on a seat just under the bank in profound calm, and a cloudless sky. I had just finished my pipe, and I was going to return to the hotel when I heard the sound of distant aeroplanes and constant gunfire, and apparently the dropping of bombs, with an occasional crash. I went up onto the parade and looking round saw crowds collected at the West End and began to see aeroplanes of which I counted more than eight, faint and white in the sunny sky nearly overhead, and heard the falling of bombs. I then returned to my old seat, as I thought I should be safer there sitting under the top of the cliff with cover above and only a very narrow place where a bomb could make a direct hit; they were falling too close to be pleasant. A soldier [- the town was full of them -] shouted 'lie down, lie down', but I saw no advantage in taking his advice.

Just then the nearest bomb fell and I saw it splash into the sea just below me. As it fell I heard it hurtling through the air quite close. The heavy guns began to roar and I saw the raiders passing in a south-easterly direction over the Straits.

Councillor John Jones in his book *Folkestone and the War*:

On May 25th 1917, at 6.10 p.m.; I had returned from tea and my usual afternoon siesta, or nap, which had been disturbed by rumbling like distant thunder in the area. Sitting comfortably in front of my shop [55 Tontine Street], I looked up to the left and perceived what seemed a spark or cigarette in the sky. This was followed by a tremendous report, such as I never heard in my life and hope to never hear again. Other sparks like rockets were seen in the air. Then an envelopment like a London fog, which lifted in a few seconds, much like a transformation scene in a pantomime. Something like the weight of an elephant seemed to sit on my knee, and then the sun broke out in all its splendour.

The sight was appalling, and beggars description. The busy crowded street, all life, was, in ten seconds, transformed into a shambles. No scene on the battlefield could have been more frightful. My leg was numbed and bleeding. I took the whole affair in at a glance, did not lose my head, and sat tight. My relative was in the shop with a neighbour opposite and they were blown some distance away. The Canadian Red Cross Ambulance party were the first to arrive, then the local fireman, police etc. The dying and the dead were being sorted out. I realised then what I had always feared, that we were not so immune from the horrors of the war as my brother councillors and tradesmen had tried to impress on the rest of the country, and I also felt that whatever the sufferings and losses were, they would teach us in future to feel for those who were daily departing for France, singing the various ditties about 'packing up their troubles in their old kit bag' etc.

The military and the police would insist I should go to the hospital for treatment. There was no necessity for this, as I told them, and there were plenty that did require attention, but they threatened force, and to appease them, I went, accompanied by my wife. An old friend of mine, Walter Banks, examined my leg and I came back, superintended clearing up the glass etc, and then a Canadian piquet would insist on taking me home, where I rested till 5 o'clock in the morning of the 26th, when I revisited the scene and stayed at the shop during the day.

Bert Prior:

We were living at 24 St John's Street – now number 26 – and my father John was on his way home from work. He was cut by glass from the window of the Mechanics Arms Hotel as he protected my brother against the wall. Mother was cut by shrapnel as she stood outside our house and neighbours had to be rescued from the debris. Our family cleared the house debris and we slept that night with the stars above us.

I saw the bombs fall on Tontine Street. I was at the upper rear windows of Graham Hill's drapers' shop at 5 High Street, where I worked as a shop boy, 11 years of age.

We boys also watched as they dug the unexploded bombs from the railway embankment between St John's Street and the Junction Station.

Doris Jones (née Prior, and sister of Bert Prior):

I was only five at the time and the raid is one of my earliest recollections. Tea had just been set out in the living room and after the bombing I remember seeing shrapnel among the bread and butter.

When we were put in a makeshift bed I was thrilled to look up and see the sky above; we had no roof.

Rosa Moseley about her mother Ruth Burvill – later Mrs Cloke:

My mum desperately wanted to go to Gosnold's in Tontine Street at the time of the raid to buy some lace at 2 ³/₄ d [about 1p] a yard. However, she was told she would have to wait until she had done the washing-up at the restaurant where she worked.

That washing-up saved her life because Gosnold's was badly damaged.

William Mitchell:

At the time of the raid I lived at Prospect Cottages on the brow of White Horse Hill on the outskirts of Hawkinge and I was on my way home after buying paraffin at the blacksmith's shop next to the pub.

As I ran home I could see a number of planes which were escorting a Zeppelin [there were no Zeppelins] lit by the setting sun high in the sky over Crete Way. I have never in all the reports of the raid heard mention of this. But the bomb that hit Tontine Street was referred to as an aerial torpedo, which in my opinion was beyond the lifting capacity of a Gotha. Being able to view it from a different angle than anyone lower down in Folkestone, I am convinced even to this day a Zeppelin was used in the raid.

My father had a florist's shop at the Central Station and as my mother had pinpointed two bombs fell there and you can imagine how concerned she was. One killed a cab driver and his horse in the approach road to the station and the other fell in Kingsnorth Gardens.

Luckily, my father had locked up the shop and gone to cut some flowers, which he grew on the allotment behind the Black Bull pub. When he returned to the shop he found that a piece of shrapnel from the Kingsnorth Gardens bomb had taken out the centre spike of the gate in the iron fence which surrounded the shop. In all probability, he would have been standing there had he not gone to pick the flowers.

William Mitchell's sister:

As each bomb dropped my mother said exactly where it fell. The thing I shall never forget is that I actually saw bombs leave the Gothas. The picture of what happened will always be clear in my mind. My mother said 'that's right in Tontine Street' and she was right.

Edward Williams:

At the time of the air raid on Folkestone in 1917, I and my brother were on our way to Vane's bakery to buy a loaf of bread. The baker's shop was opposite the old Congregational Church in Tontine Street, which has since been demolished to make way for offices.

We crossed Dover Road from Bradstone Road, where we were living at the time, and had stopped by the church on the corner to watch two Gothas approaching.

We dawdled along, eyes upturned so we shouldn't miss anything, when suddenly everything was noisy – lots of noise and dust.

I remember, people running and screaming; it was sheer pandemonium, I was very frightened, but my brother and I, as scared as we were, started to walk again towards the baker's. However, we were stopped by a man and told to run home.

I have since measured the distance from where we were standing to where the bomb had dropped – approximately 90 yards. So we were lucky.

Lilian 'Cornish' Stanley:

I was working at a store in Sandgate Road, a café and grocery store right across from the Town Hall.

I watched the planes come over and thought what a beautiful sight it was, not knowing it was the Germans until the bombs began to fall.

We all had to go to the basement until the All Clear. Then we were told to go to our homes and not to go near Tontine Street.

However, Lilian did go there, and said:

What an awful sight, I've never forgotten it.

Mrs Lily Richards and Miss Rose Hayward, twin sisters, whose mother Louisa Hayward was killed in the raid:

She was in Gosnold's shopping and was blown right over the back of Stokes Bros' greengrocery store. She was only 37 and was going shopping with me [Lily] and a friend. I asked to go back home to play, so I left her at the Dover Road end of the Tontine Street, otherwise I would have been killed.

[After the raid Lily ran down Tontine Street to find her mother:] I was turned back by a policeman. All I saw was bodies, dead horses and blood. It was terrible. I was 11 and it left us four children alone. Some friends took us in for the night.

Mrs Babs Gibbs's father, Albert Taylor, was sixteen at the time of the raid and his parents were licensees of the Brewery Tap, adjoining Stokes Bros:

He often told me how the street was like a river of blood, and arms and legs of the staff of Stokes Bros were blown on to the flat roof of the Brewery Tap.

But the most tragic thing that he remembered was the curly fair-haired head of a small child on the saloon bar step.

Years later, when my grandparents had passed on and my parents had taken over the pub; my father would scrub and whitewash the step every morning and he could still see the stain where the small head had lain.

Mrs Lily Mott was serving her apprenticeship in Gosnold's at the time:

When the bomb hit the shop I was injured but luckily not so badly as many other people were. I was buried under bodies and rubble for some hours and I have never forgotten that day.

Mrs Ellen Edwards, who with her sister, saw the Gothas fly over the viaduct:

They looked like silver birds. The sun was shining on them and they were all in formation like the letter v. Then they broke formation and started to come down and all hell broke loose. We started to run and my sister said, 'Don't look round' but I did. There were parts of people and horses in the road and fire everywhere.

We ran into a shoe shop at the end of Tontine Street – I think it was called Playfairs – and all his display tumbled down. We knew a lot of people who were killed but we didn't get a cut. I'll never forget that raid – it was awful.

Gladys Willson was working at photographer's Hawksworth Wheeler in Guildhall Street:

I was leaning out of the upstairs back room window listening to a military band practising in the drill hall.

I heard a 'whoof' but didn't know what had happened. Then we could see the bombers like silver specks. I visited the scene later and heard that a lot of people I knew had been killed.

I was 19 at the time and my boyfriend, later my husband, lived at the bottom of Tontine Street, where his father owned J T Sams, the wine merchants. Luckily damage did not reach that far.

George Turner:

I was nearly 10 years old at the time and was in the middle of Radnor Park green with my two older sisters and a youngster in a pram.

A light bi-plane – ours – flew in a wide circle and, cutting his engine slightly about 50 yards above us, he shouted to a group of soldiers and then flew off.

The soldiers reacted and ran us fast towards the park keeper's hut by Central Station. By this time all hell broke loose and my young eyes saw a terrific blast at our side of the Central Station archway and a horse and cart blow up.

Mrs K Holloway:

I was helping my father in his allotment when German planes came out of the brilliant sunshine. My father hurried me up a bank and under some trees. I saw the church clock blown out and at the top of Jointon Road a woman had her legs blown off.

Richard Pinney, then aged 9:

I was on my way home from Bouverie Square when the house at the corner of Alexandra Gardens and Bouverie Road East got one in the basement which left the house standing on two walls. A second after this bomb exploded a man's head rolled across a path and into a gutter. I didn't stop running until I got home to my parents.

Mrs A V Sharman of 32 Alexandra Gardens:

We heard explosions which we thought was some kind of practice, but the bangs came nearer and louder and we realised it was a raid. We rushed down the flights of stairs, and on going down the last flight to the basement, there was a terrific bang. The blast hit me and for a moment I could not move. All the windows had been blown out. A friend had been visiting my mother, and she went out to see what was happening. She was soon brought back with a shrapnel wound in her back. Fortunately, a nurse was soon on the scene and the victim was given immediate medical attention. Our house was third or fourth from the corner into Bouverie Road where some bombs had fallen, causing the damage to our house.

Stella Furnival:

My sister Winifred had been sent to buy something from Stokes's, but seconds after leaving, returned home saying she was scared. This probably saved her life. My mother took the basket and a few minutes later began descending the steps from St Michael's Street. As she reached the bottom of the steps she was lifted like a feather onto Tontine Street. She later described the street strewn with bodies. She was seven months pregnant, and the horror of the scene and her fear for her children made her leave this scene of carnage and return home.

Mr Ken Austin's mum, Kate, was injured in the raid:

My mother's maiden name was Kate Emily Featherbe. She was born on 14th August 1901, the daughter of James Edward and Frances Elizabeth of 30 Invicta Road, Folkestone. Her grandparents made their living from the sea fishing, while her father worked at Folkestone Harbour, unloading shipping. He also worked at Peden's Stables looking after the horses between the times the ships came into dock for unloading, and if that wasn't enough also worked part time on the rollercoaster rides!

Just three months short of her 16th birthday, my mother was caught up in the bombing, together with a Miss Pegden. Both were at the end of Tontine Street, where the road divides to go up to Grace Hill or Dover Road, and were on their way to the pier that Folkestone once had. Miss Pegden lost a leg in the blast, while my mother had all her clothes stripped off. Cut and bloodied all over, and suffering from severe shock, they were transported by horse and cart to the Royal Victoria Hospital. My mother, however, could not be admitted as the hospital was overflowing with the injured, so she had to endure another journey by horse and cart to Shorncliffe Military Hospital. It remains unbelievable they both survived.

In the same year Mother was also dealt another blow from the war. Her brother, Gunner Alfred Featherbe 168948 C Battery, 58 Brigade, Royal Field Artillery, was killed at the battle of Passchendaele on 3rd October 1917. Yet like so many others she overcame all of this and went on to raise her family through the Second World War. Furthermore she was selected and asked if she would take on the responsibility of becoming a street warden to tackle small incendiary fires. She was issued with the steel helmet, stirrup pump and buckets of sand.

Yet despite being made of steel she also had a soft   Kate Emily Featherbe
heart if the occasion arose. She assisted the midwife at the birth of any babies who were born in the Dallas Brett Crescent area. Subliminally she may have been seeking to balance things up, for she also laid out the dead!

Mrs L Peile (living in Margate, and writing in her diary for 26 May 1917):

Today we hear that a whole fleet of Taubes visited Folkestone in the afternoon and did great damage, but we have heard no details.

Mrs Coxon, describing the Folkestone raid in *Dover During the Dark Days* (1919):

My First Experience of an Air Raid. It was an exquisite summer's day in May. Some people had been having afternoon tea with me, and after they left, about 5.30, being such a perfect evening, I thought I would go and see some friends living in Earl's Avenue, so strolled out, and before I got any distance I became interested in a very large flight of about twenty aeroplanes circling and pirouetting over my head. I stopped to watch their graceful antics, and thought to myself; at last we are up and doing, fondly imagining they were our own machines practising. I leisurely walked on, and as I was crossing Earl's Avenue I noticed a woman [Mrs Bartleet] coming towards me carrying a basket. I had hardly time to reach the Olivers' garden gate when a bomb fell behind me, killing the poor woman I had just seen, and falling on the very spot of ground I had just walked over. She was picked up very shortly afterwards, but died on her way to hospital. No sooner was I in the house before

The scene outside Stokes's shop in Tontine Street just as the bomb fell is mirrored in this view of a queue outside Bayliss and Son's greengrocer's shop in Cheriton High Street in 1916. Marlinova Collection

Cheriton High Street in 1916.

another bomb crashed in Grimston Gardens, breaking all the glass of the conservatory.

There is always an uncanny 'calm' after a bomb falls, and when I could realise what had happened I at once started off to Brampton Down School to see if my daughter was safe. Going through Grimston Gardens it was exactly like walking through a thin coating of ice on a winter's day, which crackled and broke under one's feet. The roads were thickly strewn with finely-broken glass from the hundreds of windows that were smashed from the concussion, and in Grimston Gardens Tennis Courts the fall of one bomb had made a hole twenty-five feet across.

I breathed once more when I found all the girls well and safe, and greatly excited at their experience, the mistress telling me that they had behaved uncommonly well, and in doing exactly what they were told no accident had occurred.

I then telephoned to my maids at Pembury Lodge to ask if they were safe. The answer was 'yes'; but it was nothing short of Divine Providence that our house

stands today, as an aerial torpedo fell in a piece of waste ground just in front of our garden. It was a 'dud' and nothing happened, beyond some windows smashed and tiles dislodged from the roof.

Not three hundred yards away, in Kingsnorth Gardens, a lot of structural damage was done, and at the Central Railway Station two cabmen and their horses were killed outright. There is no doubt the enemy were aiming at the railway bridge, and it was exceedingly good shooting – for they only missed by a few yards. Passing over Folkestone they unfortunately got a very nice house absolutely in the centre [21 Manor Road], demolishing it to matchwood, and, alas, killing two maids who were in the kitchen at the time. The entire staircase was cut in half, and nothing remained but a heap of dust, bricks, and broken furniture. The enemy then dropped their final lot of bombs on Tontine Street, the poorer quarter of the town, near the harbour, and where crowds of *women were doing their weekend shopping. I was not there myself, but I was told afterwards by a medical man, that it resembled a battlefield – a gruesome sight of severed heads, arms, legs etc, mixed up with wreckage of broken houses and windows. Doctors and ambulances did their utmost to alleviate the awful suffering, and in a very short time every available bed in the different hospitals was filled. The exact number killed did not come out until sometime afterwards, but including Shorncliffe Camp it amounted to several hundreds and a large number of horses. In Folkestone alone the killed were 16 men, 31 women and 25 children – total 72; injured: 31 men, 43 women, 12 children – total 86. The material damage was estimated at £20,000.*

I do not think many people will be likely to forget the first visit the cultured Hun paid us on the then undefended town of Folkestone.

Chapter Nine

SCURRYING HOME IN TETHERED TRIUMPH

THE LATER EVENTS OF THE 25 MAY 1917 RAID

Leaving behind the horror in Folkestone, the bombers made for the prime target of Dover. However, the sound of the bombing in Folkestone had aroused the six army gun batteries around Dover into action and some 358 rounds were fired off. As the first of the Gothas reached the Western Heights, the air-raid sirens began to wail and naval vessels in the harbour fired off shells. Three RNAS planes were also scrambled: one from Dover, with Flight Lieutenant Reginald Leslie on board, and two from Walmer.

This first evidence of serious home defence led Brandenburg to cut his losses and abort the attack on Dover, and at around 6.35 pm he led his squadron out over

The graves of Hans Parschau and Kurt Paul Kleeman, killed when returning from the first Gotha raid on England on 25 May 1917. Thomas Genth

the Dover Strait towards home. Yet finally they were beginning to meet some opposition. Lieutenant G W Gathergood from Lympne had managed to reach the Gothas' flying height of 14,500 feet, but immediately after opening fire his Vickers gun jammed and by the time he had cleared it the Gothas were out of sight. Flight Lieutenant Leslie however, had more success: in his Sopwith Pup he managed to overhaul a lone Gotha in mid-Channel encountering engine trouble and scored direct hits, causing the plane to dive. Unfortunately, he was unable to follow the stricken bomber, as he was himself attacked by two other Gothas. In honour of his brave action, Leslie was awarded the Distinguished Service Cross.

As they approached the Belgian coast, the Gothas were to meet far more sustained action from Nos. 4 and 9 (Naval) Squadrons, which had been roused from the Dunkirk area. Indeed, one of the bombers was shot down off Dunkirk, killing *Oberleutnant* Manfred Messerschmidt, *General* von Arnim, *Leutnant* Willy

Neumann and *Leutnant* Werner Scholz, and another crashed near Beernem with *Oberleutnant* Kurt Paul Kleeman, *Leutnant* Hans Parschau and *Unteroffizier* Alfred Dickhaut perishing on board. Another was badly damaged; though it managed to limp home. These successes, minimal though they were, at least showed that sustained attacks by groups of aircraft (especially when the Gothas were low on fuel as they neared home) were a match for the enemy.

Nineteen of the Gothas returned to base and, despite the attack on London having to be aborted, the raid was seen as a great success throughout Germany and three of the pilots were decorated. A retaliatory attack on St Denis-Westrem by the British on 28 May caused damage to the airfield, but not to the Gothas themselves.

During their 1 ½-hour sortie over Britain the Gothas released 65 50kg and 104 12 ½ kg bombs, killing 96 people and, it was said, seriously injuring 195. These were the worst figures of any enemy air raid during the war up to that time, dwarfing the Zeppelin raid of 13/14 October 1915, when 71 were killed and 128 wounded.

Leutnant Hans Parschau, who was killed when his Gotha crashed at Beernem in Belgium on 25 May 1917. Thomas Genth

Chapter Ten

BRACED UP TO A
TENSION

THE AFTERMATH OF THE 25 MAY 1917 RAID

Initially the Government suppressed information about which towns had suffered during the raid. At 12.45 pm on the day after the raid (Saturday) they issued the following confusing statement:

> *A large squadron of enemy aircraft, about 16 in number, attacked the south-east of England between 5.15 and 6.30 p.m. last night. Bombs were dropped at a number of places, but nearly all the damage occurred in one town, where some of the bombs fell into the streets, causing considerable casualties amongst the civilian population. Some shops and houses were also seriously damaged.*

The net result was the swamping of the telephone system by anxious relatives wanting to know where the town was. It was only when *The Times* was permitted to carry a report from the German Official News Agency that Folkestone and

The route of the Gotha raid of 25 May 1917. Marlinova Collection

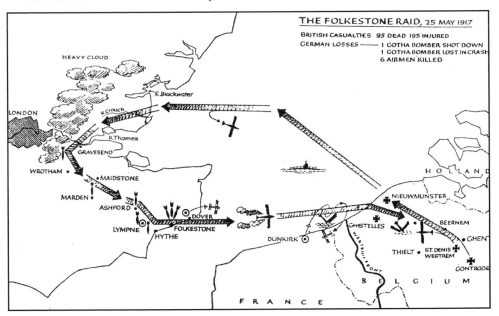

(inaccurately) Dover were said to have been hit. The secret nature of the Government report came in for great criticism and censorship was curbed for subsequent raids.

After the raid, many messages of sympathy were sent to town officials. The King and Queen sent the following message to the Mayor:

The King and Queen send deepest sympathy to the people of Folkestone in these distressing circumstances, and ask the Mayor to let the King know how the injured are progressing. The people of Folkestone have been continually in the minds of the King and Queen this last few days.

Queen Alexandra sent the following telegram:

I cannot say how deeply distressed I am at the terrible tragedy which has caused the deaths of so many harmless, innocent women and children, and which has brought such distress and suffering into so many quiet homes. Please give the poor sufferers my deepest sympathy and tell them how greatly I feel for them.

From the Lord Mayor of London:

I beg you to accept on behalf of your town the sincere sympathy of the people of London in the affliction and distress occasioned by the outrage last Friday, and request that you will convey to the bereaved and the injured the assurance that their sorrows and sufferings have evoked universal pity and commiseration throughout the community.

AIR RAID RELIEF FUND.

Subscriptions received here.

A Folkestone Air Raid Relief Fund poster.
Folkestone Library

Both the National Children's Home and Orphanage and Dr Barnardo's Homes offered to take in any children left orphaned by the raid. The Mayor of Folkestone with a subscription of £50 opened a relief fund and donations of £100 were received from Sir Philip Sassoon (the Borough Member), the Earl of Radnor, Sir Charles Wakefield and Mr J Sainsbury.

On the morning of Wednesday, 30 May 1917, a deputation of Folkestone and Hythe councillors travelled to London and, during a meeting with Lord French, Commander in Chief of Home Forces, called for adequate protection for both towns. French promised that, although German air raids could not be prevented, new defensive measures would ensure any future raids would be costly to the enemy; though this bore little relation to the state of home defences. These new measures included trained aircraft spotters aboard lightships off the east coast, increased watches on the Gotha airfields and reinforcement of the RFC Southern Home Defence Wing with up to 50 aircraft. Locally anti-aircraft guns and searchlights were placed in the town and later a machine gun was mounted on the roof of Avenue Mansions, Earls Avenue. Electric air-raid sirens were placed at the Town Hall and Fire Station in Dover Road, and steam sirens at the Public Baths in Foord Road and the Electricity Works at Morehall. Ten short blasts would warn of an air raid (nine according to John Jones) and one long blast sounded the all-clear: it is said the sirens could be heard 10 miles away! John Jones commented:

Jerry [or] *Fritz was not very polite or regular in announcing his visits, and this caused me, among others a little inconvenience. The sirens gave nine blasts; the sirens on the steamers approaching the harbour gave four blasts from the ship coming from the French port and three for another. Hence it was a little confusing. You would get four; then a pause. Breathe again; then three, then a pause. Hardly having recovered, you would hear nine. Then it was 'down tools' and 'up shelters'.*

Stanley Coxon described one such air-raid scare:

We were out shopping one fine morning in the car when the siren sounded. At the time I was sitting in the car, while my wife was in a greengrocer's shop making the daily purchases. It was in Sandgate Road, 'the' public thoroughfare of the place, when a man crossed into the middle of the street and stood there peering skywards, with a pair of binoculars. A nervous, excitable lady, seeing him in this position, rushed across to him and asked him where they were. Stretching his arms towards the sky and extending them outwards, he replied in the most lugubrious howl ever howled, 'Madame, they're all over England!' Exit the [lady] *at a hand gallop! As our kids were on the beach bathing, we decided to hurry home – which was on our way – drop our purchases and go for them. Ahead of us, ambling along for all they* [were] *worth, were two maiden ladies, evidently sisters, and both bound for the same refuge of safety. Just as we approached the corner of the street, a constable flew round on a bike, blowing a fearsome whistle and displaying a large placard with the ominous warning: 'Air Raid. Clear the Streets. Take Shelter.' The suddenness of the apparition, combined with the shock of the signal, was clearly too much for the nerves of two poor souls, who immediately dropped all their parcels in the middle of the road, and galloped off in opposite directions!*

Dugouts and shelters were provided at the top of Marshall Street, the rear of Mead Road, the sandpit north of Radnor Park, in the basement of unfinished houses in Cheriton Road, Morehall, Mr Scrivener's Coal Stores (under Radnor Bridge Arch), Darlington Arch and the old lime kiln at Killick's Corner. After an alarm had been received, the basement of the Town Hall, the Technical School, Sidney Street Schools, the Harvey Grammar School, a new garage on the Bayle and a store under Mr Reason's house were all added to the list. The Martello tunnel was also an addition, the railway line to Dover having been closed by a landslip in the Warren in December 1915. Yet a military expert later reported that many of the shelters would not have afforded much protection from a direct hit. In the event the new defence measures were to be little tested as the only other raid that came near Folkestone was an evening attack on 25/26 September 1917 when all the bombs fell outside the town, including two on Castle Hill and three on the waterworks. Hostile aircraft and Zeppelins were to pass harmlessly over the town on seven further occasions between September and December 1917; during the final occasion on 18 December a Gotha was hit in the petrol tank by guns at Westenhanger. As it tried to make its way home across the Channel the plane came down 3 miles off Folkestone Harbour and its two surviving crew, after sending distress signals, were picked up by a trawler. However, just as the crew of the trawler were preparing to bring the wrecked Gotha aboard it was blown up by a time-fused bomb and one of the trawlermen, 47-year-old Frank Gee, suffered serious injuries to which he succumbed the following day. The two prisoners were landed at Folkestone Harbour and were sent to London under escort. There were 20 further air-raid warnings in 1918, the last on 24 August, but no actual enemy action took place on the town.

A solemn memorial service in memory of those killed in the raid was held at Folkestone Parish Church on Saturday, 2 June 1917, led by the Archbishop of Canterbury, Dr Randall Davidson. During the service, held between 12 and 2 pm, all shops in the town were closed. On the following day, an outdoor service held in Radnor Park by the United Churches of Folkestone attracted a huge crowd.

Yet Folkestone's aura as a safe haven had been shattered and after the raid many of the remaining private schools were closed and further residents left the district. Visitors shunned the town. Feelings against local people of German origin ran high, fanned by the words of local councillor Robert Forsyth, who felt they should be interned without delay and their businesses closed down. He rammed home the point during a large rally at the Hippodrome site, Linden Crescent. J Crowhurst summed up the state of affairs:

The Mayor of Folkestone (Sir Stephen Penfold) and Sir Philip Sassoon, Borough MP, leave the Town Hall to attend one of the memorial services. Folkestone Herald

FOLKESTONE
PARISH CHURCH.

𝔐emorial
Service

FOR

ALL WHO LOST THEIR LIVES IN
THE RECENT AIR-RAID
ON FRIDAY. MAY 25th. 1917.

Saturday, June 2nd, 1917,
at 12.15 p.m.

BEWLEY
PRINTER. FOLKESTONE

Borough of Folkestone.

AIR RAID.

In Memoriam Service

IN

RADNOR PARK,

On SUNDAY, June 3rd, 1917, at 3 o'clock.

Rev. J. E. HARLOW (Wesleyan Church) presiding.

ATTENDED BY HIS WORSHIP THE MAYOR
(LIEUT.-COL. SIR STEPHEN PENFOLD, J.P.).

And Members of the Corporation.

REPRESENTATIVES OF HIS MAJESTY'S FORCES.

And PUBLIC BODIES.

Order of Service.

Selection by Band 18th Reserve C.E.F. (by kind permission
of Lieut.-Col. Bedson),

Hymn I.

All people that on earth do dwell,
Sing to the Lord with cheerful voice;
Him serve with fear, His praise forth
tell,
Come ye before Him, and rejoice.

The Lord, ye know, is God indeed;
Without our aid He did us make;
We are His flock, He doth us feed,
And for His sheep He doth us take.

O enter then His gates with praise,
Approach with joy His courts unto;
Praise, laud, and bless His Name
always,
For it is seemly so to do.

For why? the Lord our God is good;
His mercy is for ever sure;
His truth at all times firmly stood,
And shall from age to age endure.
Amen.

*The programme covers for the two memorial services for the Folkestone raid held on 2
and 3 June 1917.* Folkestone Library

*There was a change in the local atmosphere. Gone was our complacency; gone was
that feeling of security and immunity with which we had previously pursued the
even tenure of our way. The war had been brought home to us with a fierce intensity.
There was no actual panic, but the populace was braced up to a tension which it had
not known before (and which would last to the war's end).*

Councillor John Jones added:

*The town more or less got 'jumpy', nerve-racked, and quite made up in excitement
for their previous apathy. Everybody seemed to have different ideas of protecting the
town; in fact, a large number lost their heads entirely. A still-greater number flew
away and left us in our glory. The husbands said it was their wives and children who
insisted on their going while the wives said they did not mind, but it was their
husbands who became so worried. The net result was that they went to the west or
north or somewhere else.*

The people of Folkestone became increasingly hungry as 1917 wore on, because of
food shortages and strict controls on what little there was. To throw rice at a
wedding became an offence and luxuries such as chocolates and cakes were
limited to a sale of 2oz, with some grocers selling others, such as sugar and jam, to
registered customers only. The Government regulated bread and filled it with
ingredients such as barley, maize, rice, beans, oatmeal and potato. Sugar eventually

became the first food for which ration cards were issued and long queues outside the food shops became the norm as more items became rationed. By February 1918, butter, margarine and meat became impossible to purchase in Folkestone without a ration card. The allowance was 1 $\frac{1}{2}$ lb of meat per head per week for adults (10oz for children under ten); butter or margarine 4oz and sugar 8oz. Tea and jam were also rationed and even potatoes for a time were limited to 1lb per week. Yet as Miss Peel summed up:

> By the end of July 1918 the public knew that all fear of starvation owing to the German blockade was ended, but that supplies must continue to be limited and prices remain high. Considering the suffering and discomfort due to the shortages of food and fuel, overwork, personal unhappiness and a general mental strain, the people as a whole remained wonderfully calm. They grumbled, but their grumbling was chiefly an emotional outlet. Directly they understood the position, though they might still grumble, there remained the determination to 'stick it' to do their bit to win the war.

Chapter Eleven

FURTHER FLIGHTS OF FEARLESS DARE

THE OTHER DAYLIGHT GOTHA RAIDS, JUNE TO AUGUST 1917

The Second Gotha Daylight Raid
Tuesday, 5 June 1917 (16.00-21.00 hours) on Shoeburyness and Sheerness.
22 planes, 74 bombs; casualties: 3 civilians killed, 9 injured; 10 military killed, 25 injured.
1 Gotha shot down by AA fire (Barton's Point).

Additional fuel tanks fitted to the bombers meant the Nieuwmunster fuel strip was not now necessary. In addition escort fighters accompanied the Gothas on the last half-hour of the return flight to Belgium. A more northerly course was taken by the bombers to avoid being seen by the RNAS at Dunkirk, yet they were to be harassed across the North Sea by three Pups from No. 4 (Naval) Squadron. The Gothas crossed the River Crouch at 6.15 pm and attacked the Army's gunnery establishment at Shoeburyness, killing two soldiers. Accurate AA fire from the Artillery School dispersed the planes and the London objective was abandoned.

The naval dockyard town of Sheerness, 6 miles across the Thames Estuary, was then targeted, but two bombers at this point dropped out and flew back, possibly because of engine trouble. During the five-minute raid, thirty-two 50kg and thirteen 12 $^1/_2$ kg bombs fell on Sheerness, mainly hitting military targets, though three civilians were killed. One 12 $^1/_2$ kg bomb demolished the back of a house in Invicta Road and another partially wrecked the Crown and Anchor and the Pier Hotel in the High Street. Messrs Grieves gentlemen's outfitters was hit by two bombs, causing the death of the 27-year-old shop manager Edward Perry (who had just returned from visiting his sick wife in Plymouth) and customer Samuel Hawes, a Chief Warrant Officer aboard HMS *Actaeon* who lived at 129 Alexandra Road. Four workmen from Messrs R Corben and Co. of Maidstone, who were carrying out work in the shop, were injured, particularly E Piper, who was blown down into the basement with all his clothes torn off. Three further military fatalities were caused by a 50kg bomb that fell in the moat 400 yards south-west of Ravelin Bridge, and in all, eight military personnel were killed.

Nine-year-old Stephen Keen, who lived near the railway station, where his father worked in the signal box, witnessed the raid:

I was playing cricket with other youngsters in a field a short way from the railway line and about fifty yards from the signal box; I remember it being a beautiful day with no cloud. The AA guns started firing and my friends scuttled home, but being

the clever one I stayed and watched the planes, with my father almost frantic, calling
for me to go home. I had not seen anything so fascinating as this in my life before,
and was really absorbed, the planes were not a great height and I could plainly see
the way they delivered the bombs, by hand, over the side. Most of them dropped in
the water and from where I was standing I suppose the angle was about forty-five
degrees. I don't know the number of planes which took part, but I counted six or
seven when it happened – it was the last I knew of the raid until a long time
afterwards, for as I was looking up I caught a shell splinter in my eye.

Stephen lost the sight of that eye and also suffered from poor hearing for the
remainder of his life.

Mrs Valerie Simmons's grandfather, George Frier (50), was killed in the raid and
she remembered:

He was the father of six children, the youngest of whom was my father, then aged
ten. He worked in Sheerness Dockyard as a rigger, and went outside his workplace
with friends to see what was going on, whereupon he was hit by shrapnel and killed.
The other person killed was a man [Herbert Lucas from Gillingham] who lived in
Cavour Road, who was hit in or near a walkway called Dutchell's Opening, where, I
believe, the marks of the shrapnel are still visible.

The Naval Dockyard was naturally a target and one 50kg bomb struck a
warehouse known as the 'Grand Store' and burnt it out in a blaze lasting over two
hours. The bomb that killed Mr Frier had narrowly missed a ship in No. 3 Dock.

Accurate fire from the Barton's Point AA hit one of the Gothas and it crashed
into the sea close to the Nore Lightship. The pilot, Eric Kluck, was drowned (the
first Gotha crew member to die in action over England), and *Leutnant* Hans
Francke died the next day, though the third crew member, *Unteroffizier* Georg
Schumacher, survived.

After an unsuccessful attempt to bomb the power station and airship sheds at
Minster (Sheppey), the Gothas made for home. Over Belgium they were attacked
by RNAS Nos 4 and 9 (Naval) Squadrons and three of the escort fighters were shot
down.

The Third Gotha Daylight Raid

Wednesday, 13 June 1917 (09.00-14.00 hours) on Margate, Shoeburyness, London
(Docks, East End and City).
22 planes (20 crossed the English coast), 128 bombs; casualties: 158 (2 by AA fire)
civilians killed, 425 (18 by AA fire) injured; 4 military killed, 7 injured, 1 British
observer killed.

The order rescinding the prevention of inland batteries firing was given on
Thursday, 7 June 1917. An earlier attack time was planned in order to maximize the
propaganda effects of a raid on London and to avoid possible late-afternoon
thunderstorms. Two Gothas soon developed engine trouble and returned home,
but when the others reached the North Foreland one raider diverted to attack
Margate as a diversionary measure. Four or five 50kg bombs were dropped on the
town; around 100 houses were damaged in the Tivoli Road area and four people
slightly injured, but thirteen home aircraft were lured away from the main raiding
party. Two further Gothas peeled off to attack Shoeburyness, dropping five 50kg
bombs and injuring two civilians, and another to photograph military

establishments. The familiar two-flights-abreast configuration of Gothas then approached the east of the capital, hidden by a patchy layer of cloud that made them harder to spot from the ground. Barking, East Ham (4 killed) and Silvertown (18 killed) were all attacked before 72 bombs were released on residential districts within a mile of Liverpool Street Station. Three bombs landed on the station itself killing 16, and further fatalities occurred at 65 Fenchurch Street (20 killed), Aldgate High Street (13) and a foundry at Beech Court (8). The most tragic incident of the raid occurred when 18 children were killed and 30 terribly mutilated by a direct hit on the Upper North Street School, Poplar. Across the river, there were further fatalities in Bermondsey and Southwark. Despite harassment by British aircraft and AA fire, all the Gothas returned safely home before the threatened thunderstorm broke.

Leutnant Walter Aschoff, a close friend of Adolf Genth who had luckily survived a crash-landing after the attack on Folkestone, took part in this raid and later described it in his book *Londonflüge 1917*:

> *A view back to Kollberg [the pilot], so that's it - let's go! The throttles are moved to the full throttle position, a shaking and vibration is going through the body of the bird and also through us and with gathering speed we are rushing over the ground with our heavy load, lift off! Gliding, flying into heaven and to far away shores – and*

The classroom of the Upper North Street School, Poplar where 18 children were killed during the Gotha raid on London on 13 June 1917. Marlinova Collection

maybe we are flying into our death.

The sun is shining, through the haze to the east I can see – like shadows – the aircraft of other squadrons. We are flying a long turn, building formations, at first groups, but finally we become united and fly altogether heading to our target in wing flight formation. We are looking like a swarm of birds, which is flying towards an unknown country.

The heading for the moment is northbound, river and channels are blinking up and glittering, and over the meadows there is still a slight fog to be seen. Old little towns wake up from their dreams, villages appear from the nicely coloured Flandric province and disappear while new pictures catch the eye. We are getting more and more close to the coastline, even now – still far away – the long beach can be seen glimmering.

At 3,000 metres (9,840 feet) we are high above the entrance to Zeebrugge. From here we are on standby; the torpedo boats lying below should help us in the case of a crash-landing in the water, the black smoke trails are moving to the south-west. Far – endless far, we are looking over the open sea.

From time to time my eyes meet with the ones of my pilot, checking the engines and wings, a signal wakes up the rear gunner hanging onto his thoughts. Other aircraft are dancing close to us, flying over and near under us, so that it is necessary to pay attention to prevent a crash with them, which could send us down before reaching the target.

Meanwhile we have reached an altitude of 4,500 metres (14,760 feet), just in the middle above the North Sea bay running to the south-west under us. Because of the good visibility today, the view is moving without any limits. Is that not a piece of land there far away, English land, which we are not searching with our souls, but with our strong will to fight.

We are closing in; north-west there is to be seen the steep coastline, which we are approaching, to the north my eyes are looking far over Harwich. Moving southward, until they find the delta of the big River Thames, Margate and Ramsgate appear, the white cliffs are gleaming to us until they are interrupted by Dover and Folkestone. I am bending to the rear left and perceive Dunkirk and Calais and above the waters of the channel, streaming to the ocean. Behind us the sun has reached her midday position and it looks like she is greeting us friendly. Finally I have some time to look to the south-east over the Dutch islands, then our thoughts and eyes are fixed to the things ahead of us.

Suddenly a lot of great and small boats are swimming in the colour changing sea. Warships are changing rapidly their directions, because they are afraid of our bombs, leaving light trails of moving water behind them. We look at them with a smile: our bombs today are for a better target. South-east of Harwich a convoy of more than twenty merchant ships accompanied by torpedo boats and destroyers to protect them against submarines is heading north.

The countryside is getting bigger and bigger, every detail is clearly visible now. Outpost boats and then anti aircraft artillery opens fire at us, most likely the men behind this guns are cursing against us flying high above them. Little white and grey clouds are suddenly in the air, vanishing slowly and covering again the sky. This means nothing to the 'old' crew members, they are used to the smoke of guns and the noise of exploding grenades.

The soil of the until now unreachable and safe island is flown over in bright daylight by a wing flight of German bombers. The feeling of a great unique event fills our chests and the heartbeat gets higher and our eyes are shining. We are leaving the Thames area and set course directly to the northern part of London.

In the green land appears a dark, black and grey coloured area; it grows and grows like our close attention. There are thousands of houses, hundreds of streets, places coming together, forming the giant city of London. We are above the northern part of the town; the leading airplane is turning to the south now. Railway stations, factories and depots look like little toys. To the east at the many channels and little rivers of the Thames there are big dockyards to be seen. From the big 'stone mass' there is especially outstanding the tower; the St. Paul's Cathedral and the Bank of England.

The anti aircraft fire of the batteries in and around London has started now with great power. Grenade explosions cover the cloudless sky, the noise of the explosions are – when close – sometimes stronger than the noise of the engines. This forces our aircraft to turn and to go down, threatening sometimes to tear apart our formation.

We are flying 5,000 metres (16,400 feet) above London, a very strong impression for us, something indescribable. How about the people down there, in which hurry and fear will they be now, looking desperately for some place to hide?

Another airplane beside me is dropping his bombs. I also found my target and show my pilot the direction he should fly. A big area with docks and stores is under us, I take the lever, which will release the bombs and one after the other is falling into the depth.

A strong jerk follows every drop. Our aircraft climbs rapidly. I have to clasp myself at my chair; I am shaken and was nearly thrown out of the plane. Finally I am standing again and watch the impacts. It looks like the target was hit, smoke and fire is coming out of the halls.

While standing and watching, I suddenly hear a strange rattle. Enemy aircraft attacking us! Machine gun fire from the rear gunner and me is our answer. In a few seconds my first drum is empty and I try to load a new one, not that simple in an aircraft that fast. New rounds are fired and I can see due to the phosphor trails that they are reaching the fighter. The enemy goes into a steep dive. Did he quit because he was hit, or he gave up because our fire was coming too close to him, we will never find out.

We leave London behind; still the smoke and haze can be seen forming big clouds over the town. In this stress, we are hardly thinking of the people living in this town, people like us, with blood like ours. And this thought should not affect us, it is war, hard war, it takes our whole power to fight.

We are crossing airfields, where fighters start to catch us and we see everywhere the fire of the anti aircraft guns. The whole of southern England seems to be alerted. We are flying as quickly as possible to reach the coastline and soon there is the good old sea below us.

The aircraft are flying high level in formation again to reach the home base. A sign of the rear gunner makes me look behind us; he is aiming at an aircraft coming from the direction of Southend, one of the feared English triplanes. The enemy fighter pilot seems not to be a big hero, or he is too careful coming close to the formation. We hear his machine guns far away and gave him some bullets in front of his nose.

Our eyes are looking forward again. There! The white houses of Ostend appear in the haze, far behind it the terrible battlefield of Flanders. In 15 minutes we will be overhead the country and safe. German fighters will accompany us and bring us home safely. I am searching the sky and show my pilot and the rear gunner some dark points, which I believe are our fighters.

Our heavy engines are singing their special song, which I will never forget. I am always trying to give some words to this song, but I never found some.

The mysterious dark points at the horizon are becoming aircraft and when they get closer, I can suddenly see the cockades of one of them, the enemy! They are coming in quick from the front side; I grasp my machine gun and make some sign to the rear gunner that there is danger ahead, press the gun at my shoulder, aim and start firing. A few moments later we are under attack from the rear above. A Sopwith fighter jumped down on us until he is only 50 metres away and starts shooting at our Gotha.

Trails of phosphor are coming closer to us and they are hitting holes into the wing. Without a break the rear gunner is firing at the enemy. The attack is over; the rear gunner is already taking his second gun and tries to destroy the fighter through his downward 'tunnel'. I am creeping to him and provide him with new drums of ammunition, the only thing I can do now – with my gun I cannot reach the enemy plane now.

The pilot is working nervously at the gasoline cock, the engines are running roughly, but suddenly the sound gets normal, the gravity tank is intact, both others are hit and empty.

We see other German aircraft getting closer; they saw the situation and came to protect us from the enemy fighter. With the last fuel we reach our base and give the distress signal to land immediately. The aircraft is now free of the bombs and fuel, which means it is difficult to handle. We are thrown up and down and once again the pilot has to be fully concentrated at the end of our five hours flight. A task some inexperienced pilots have failed. At the northern edge of the airfield, close to a single farm we see a crashed plane. Then we see another aircraft lying burning on the ground. Maybe it hit a crater from a bomb attack that took place while we were in the air. But these impressions must be blocked out now, if we want to land safely.

We are coming down more and more, hangars and trees growing suddenly out of the ground, people become taller – we are short before touch down, Kollberg pushes the plane with high speed down to the ground, the wheels have contact some little unevenness, the last moving, we have landed!

The raid was a great success for the Germans and Brandenburg was presented by the Kaiser with the *Pour le Mérite* cross. The *Lokalanzeiger* commented:

The bloodthirsty rage produced in England by the success of the attack on 'fortified London', is only one more proof of its success. The British and French attacks on German unfortified towns are revolting and murderous, but the German attacks on fortified towns like London are completely permissible as military undertakings. If the British wish to return the Germans' visit in a fair and honourable way, they must attack the German fortresses and fortified places. They know quite well they do not.

The Times, as expected, took a different view:

The raid slew women and children as well as men. It wrecked buildings of no greater military value than a warehouse here, a tobacconist's shop there and a school not far away. If it were possible at this time of day to increase the utter and most detestation with which he [the Kaiser] *is held by the people of this country, he did it today.*

It was during this raid that the famous Gillingham fighter ace James McCudden VC had his first brush with the Gothas (he was to meet them again on 7 July 1917). The top British fighter ace of the war with 57 confirmed kills, McCudden was serving as an instructor at Joyce Green, Dartford and recalled in his book *Flying Fury*:

> On the morning of the 13th I left Joyce Green in my Pup, to fly to Croydon to give a lecture. I arrived at Croydon after fifteen minutes' flying and taxied up to the sheds, and noticed that everyone seemed rather excited. I got out of my machine just as the CO came and told me that a hostile formation of aeroplanes had crossed the coast and were making for London. I was much annoyed, for my Lewis gun and ammunition were at Joyce Green, and to get them meant wasting valuable time. However, I got off the ground again and made an average of 105 miles per hour from Croydon to Joyce Green. In fifteen minutes I landed there, and while taxiing in I noticed some German prisoners who were employed on the aerodrome seemed to be very pleased with life, and were all looking aloft. I got out of my Pup, yelled to my mechanics to bring my gun and ammunition and, while we were putting the gun on, I could plainly hear the roar of the many engines of the Hun formation which had just passed over.
>
> Towards Woolwich I could hear the occasional bang of an English Archie, but I could not see the Huns at all as there was an irregular layer of woolly clouds at about 5,000 feet which blocked one's view. The overlap of the exhaust of the many powerful engines sounded very formidable and, judging by the noise, I was certain that there was over a dozen machines. In a minute my machine was ready, and I took off in an easterly direction, towards the south of the Thames. At 5,000 feet I climbed into the woolly clouds, and not until I had

Gillingham's hero and the top British fighter ace of the war, James McCudden VC, pictured in 1918 with his dog, Bruiser. McCudden had a couple of encounters with the Gothas. Marlinova Collection

> reached 10,000 feet did I see the ground again through the small gaps between the clouds. It was an ideal day for a bombing formation to get their objective unobserved. When I again was able to note my position I found myself over Chatham. I still flew east and arrived over Sheerness at 13,000 feet. My mind was now divided as to which way the Huns would return, and I conjectured that they would fly SE from Chatham

over Kent, so I still climbed, and when I got to 15,000 feet, still over Sheppey, I caught the flash of a gun from Southend, and looking upwards saw a characteristic black and white British Archie bursting over Shoeburyness at about my own height. I increased my speed at once and flew in a direction east of the Archie and, after a few minutes, could distinguish a lot of machines in good formation going towards the south-east. I caught up to them at the expense of some height, and by the time I had got under the rear machine I was 1,000 feet below. I now found that there were over twenty machines, all with two 'pusher' engines. To my dismay I found that I could not lessen the range to any appreciable extent. By the time I had got to 500 feet under the rear machine we were twenty miles east of the Essex coast, and visions of a very long swim entered my mind, so I decided to fire all my ammunition and then depart. I fired my first drum, of which the Hun did not take the slightest notice. I now perceived another Sopwith Pup just behind this rear Hun at quite close range, but after a while he turned away as though he was experiencing some trouble with his gun. How insolent did those damned Boches look, absolutely lording the sky above England! I replaced my first drum with another and had another try, after which the Huns swerved ever so slightly, and then that welcome sound of machine guns smote my ears and I caught the smell of the Huns' incendiary bullets as they passed me. I now put on my third and last single Lewis drum and fired again and, to my intense chagrin, the last Huns did not take the slightest notice. I now turned west and the coast of Kent looked only a blur, for although I was over 14,000 feet the visibility was very poor. On the way back to Joyce Green, I was absolutely furious to think that the Huns should come over and bomb London and have it practically their own way. I simply hated the Hun more than ever. I landed at Joyce Green after having been in the air for over two hours, and I was very dispirited, cold and bad-tempered, but after I had had lunch and a glass of port, I thought that life after all wasn't so bad.

James Thomas Byford 'Jimmie' McCudden VC, DSO and Bar, MC and Bar, Military Medal and *Croix de Guerre*, was born on 28 March 1895 into a family of Irish Catholics with a distinguished military service history. Both Jimmie's father and grandfather had served in the army, and in 1910, aged 15, he became a bugler in the Royal Engineers, who were based just a few hundred yards from his home at Brompton Barracks. In 1913 he enlisted in the RFC as a mechanic and with the coming of war the following year he was promoted to Flight Sergeant. He claimed his first kill in September 1916, for which he was given the Military Medal, and went on to win the Military Cross in February 1917, to which a Bar was added in August 1917.

Jimmie's impeccable flying attributes of quick reactions, aggression and dash led him to take command of B Flight of 56 Squadron in France, and flying his SE5a took them into combat with the mighty Red Baron Manfred von Richthofen. He was involved in the shooting-down of another top German fighter ace, Werner Voss, on 23 September 1917.

On 2 April 1918 Jimmie was awarded the Victoria Cross, and Gillingham honoured its most famous son by granting him the freedom of the Borough. Sadly, before he was able to personally except the award, Jimmie's plane suffered engine failure on take-off at Aux-le-Chateau, France on 9 July 1918 and crashed into trees. He suffered a fractured skull and died two hours later. The body was laid to rest in Wavans Cemetery, though his name was added to the McCudden family memorial

Ibion Hill, Ramsgate, which was vice wrecked by Zep. Bombs on ay 17th, 1915, & June 17th, 1917.

A young lady holds a 'souvenir' from the Imperial Bazaar on Albion Hill, which proudly proclaims it was wrecked twice by Zep bombs on 17 May 1915 and 17 June 1917. Marlinova Collection

The houses in Albert Road, Ramsgate, wiped out by an aerial torpedo during the Dump Raid of 17 June 1917. Three of the occupants were killed. Marlinova Collection

in Chatham Cemetery.

Four days after the devastation of the London Raid, a squad of six Zeppelins (L42, L44-48) showed that they were still a threat. On the night of 16/17 June 1917 L42 (LZ91) abandoned a raid on London because of bad weather and made instead for Ramsgate and Dover. At 2 am the first two aerial torpedoes were dropped on Ramsgate: one landed harmlessly in the sea, but the other landed squarely on an ammunition dump, located in a converted fish market by the harbour. The resulting explosion damaged 660 houses in the town and smashed around 10,000 sheets of glass.

A sheet of blood-red flame shot upwards and for hours ammunition of all kinds continued to explode with a tornado of fury. As the spreading flames of the blazing mass sent a gorgeous glow of colour into the sky, the rumour spread inland that the whole of Ramsgate was on fire and as the fury of the explosions became intensified many of the inhabitants themselves believed the enemy were attempting a landing.

The 'Dump Raid', as it became known, claimed three lives, Benjamin Thouless and Jonathan and Mrs Hamlyn, when an aerial torpedo demolished four houses in Albert Road. Sixteen others were injured as Crescent Road, Southwood House, Ivy Lane, Addington Street and Manston were all hit. Douglas G Evans was in Ramsgate that night and remembered:

Raids followed at fairly frequent intervals. I recall one especially bad night when, from the dining room, which had French windows, we stared out into the darkness. Suddenly a dull red arc of light lit half the sky silhouetting nearby houses and trees. A few seconds passed – then once again the sky was alight with fire. This time the arc was bigger, a glaring red, flecked with black streaks. There was the sound of a terrific explosion. This time the nearby houses were not silhouetted; they were blown to smithereens. Four of them in a row were utterly destroyed, an aerial torpedo passing through the lot.

Almost before the glare of that explosion had died down, the whole town, it seemed, became a shaking world: doors rattled and slammed; the night had become a blaze of flashing lights of every colour. A bomb had struck the ammunition dump on Ramsgate Harbour.

The town was paralysed for days, with a third of it shut off to the public while the big clear-up was undertaken. Dover, on the other hand, escaped unscathed as its two bombs fell into the harbour.

The Fourth Gotha Daylight Raid

Wednesday, 4 July 1917 (05.30-09.00 hours) on Harwich and Felixstowe.
25 planes (18 crossed the English coast), 65 bombs; casualties: 3 civilians killed, 1 injured; 14 military killed, 28 injured, 1 British observer killed.
1 Gotha badly damaged.

Rudolf Kleine, a Prussian with a successful military career, was now the commander of the Gotha squadron after Brandenburg sustained serious injuries in a crash on 19 June 1917, just a few days after his meeting with the Kaiser. Kleine was a rather impetuous man who was determined to better Brandenburg's so-far impressive results, yet he had an inauspicious start when, shortly after the start of this his first raid, seven of the Gothas had to return to base because of engine trouble. As the squadron reached the Suffolk coast a lone DH4 attacked them, but

The crash of Gotha GIV (LVG) 395/16 with commander Leutnant *Noack and pilot* Leutnant *Wittee on board. The plane came down near Ghent on 20 June 1917.*
Thomas Genth

its gunner was killed and the pilot had to call off the engagement. The right-hand wing of the Gothas attacked Harwich and the left-hand wing Felixstowe, where the RNAS station was attacked with the loss of six naval ratings and three civilian workmen. The other casualties included three naval personnel at Shotley balloon station and five soldiers of the 3rd Battalion, Suffolk Regiment. One Gotha was badly damaged on the way home when British fighters attacked the squadron.

The Fifth Gotha Daylight Raid
Saturday, 7 July 1917 (08.00-13.00 hours) on Margate, London (north-east and City).
24 planes (22 crossed the English coast), 76 bombs; casualties: 55 (10 by AA fire)
civilians killed, 190 (55 by AA fire) injured; 2 military killed, 3 injured.
1 Gotha destroyed in combat, 4 crashed on landing; 2 British aircraft destroyed, 2 pilots killed.
Once more a single Gotha peeled off from the main thrust to attack Margate and RNAS Manston, where three 50kg bombs destroyed three houses, and three people were killed. At 11 Arundel Road, one bomb completely wrecked the house, killing James Marks, his wife and her lady companion Miss A M Cooper. Another fell in the back garden of 7 Princes Avenue, demolishing the rear of the premises, and Northdown Road and Crawford Gardens were also hit. The plane managed to avoid 115 rounds of AA fire before returning back.

The main body of the squadron approached London from the north-east and a bomb dropped in Boleyn Road, Stoke Newington killed nine people. Thirty bombs landed on the City, causing great material damage and thirteen fatalities, and a bomb that fell on Tower Hill killed eight people. The GPO's Central Telegraph Office in St Martin's-le-Grand was largely destroyed and a soldier was killed, while six people perished in the area close to St Bartholomew's Hospital and four

The Gotha GIV 406/16, now with the initials 'RG' (Radke/Genth), shortly before reaching London on the 7 July 1917 raid. Thomas Genth

close to the river in Lower Thames Street. The Gothas were rarely bothered by the inaccurate AA fire (which killed ten civilians) and easily beat off any lone home fighters over the capital. However, on the return flight (after bombing south and east London) they were harried by several aircraft, including James McCudden's Sopwith Pup.

One of the Gothas was brought down in the sea, its crew of three – *Leutnant* Max Eisner, *Vizefeldwebel* Franz Holger and *Unteroffizier* Georg Michel – all perishing, while a further four crash-landed on the airfields and were written off. The crew of one Gotha that perished at St Denis-Westrem were *Leutnant* Max Roselmüller, *Leutnant* Hans Richter and *Vizefeldwebel* Wilhelm Weber. The raid was the most successful in terms of material damage with many warehouses destroyed at a cost of £205,622.

The Sixth Gotha Daylight Raid
Sunday, 22 July 1917 (06.30-10.00 hours) on Harwich and Felixstowe.
23 planes (22 crossed the English coast), 55 bombs; casualties: 1 civilian killed, 3 injured; 12 military killed, 23 injured.
1 Gotha shot down in the sea off Ostend, 2 British aircraft damaged by AA fire.
After the second raid on London, an ugly mood developed for anything remotely German, including the Royal Family, whose surname (Saxe-Coburg-Gotha) included the name of the murderous bomber. On 17 July 1917 they wisely changed it to Windsor. One of the aims of the raids was for the British public to call for peace, but the overwhelming cry was for retaliation against German cities (which

was not to occur until the final months of the war). A thorough organization of Home Defence was carried out under General Jan Smuts which addressed the need for a unity of command, more AA guns (including a ring around London) and day-fighting aircraft squadrons and a reserve force. A new air-raid warning system was to be used for London.

The next Gotha raid returned to Harwich and Felixstowe, but the formation was disrupted by good AA fire. Nevertheless 55 bombs were dropped on the two towns, Felixstowe and its RNAS station once again being the main target. Aside from a lone home fighter, the Gothas were not harassed until they reached the Dunkirk area, where one was brought down. A bizarre sequel to this raid occurred in London when the red alert was given in error and maroon rockets were set off. AA batteries in the south Essex area assumed the raiders were in the area and began firing at their own craft, bringing two of them down.

The Seventh Gotha Daylight Raid

Sunday, 12 August 1917 (14.30-19.30 hours) on Margate, Rochford, Leigh, and Southend. 13 planes (10 crossed the English coast), 37 bombs; casualties: 32 civilians killed, 43 injured; no military killed, 2 injured. 1 Gotha destroyed in combat, 1 crash-landed at Zeebrugge, 4 crashed on landing.

A raid had been aborted over the North Sea on 29 July 1917 because of bad weather and throughout August the conditions were to be the worst for fifty years. A rare glimpse of the sun on the morning of 12 August 1917 led to an impulsive decision by Kleine to attack London that afternoon, though the leader himself stayed at home and Richard Walter led the attack. The suddenness of his decision meant only thirteen planes were available for the raid and three of them soon had to turn back because of engine failure. Margate was once again a target for a single bomber, who dropped four bombs, damaging forty buildings and injuring one woman, before making for home. The lone Margate raider was besieged all the way by British fighters and lost the use of an engine before crash-landing at Zeebrugge.

The main force dropped three bombs on Rochford Airfield, but the attack on London had to be aborted because of the dark rain-clouds lying over the capital, and the Southend area was targeted instead. Unfortunately, the popular holiday town (which was crowded with holidaymakers) had no air-raid warning system and thirty-four bombs (about half were duds) were dropped on both Leigh and Southend. Thirty-two people were killed and forty-three injured, mainly in the centre of Southend, the worst instance being when a 50kg bomb exploded amongst pedestrians in crowded Victoria Avenue, close to the railway station, killing fifteen. Sustained AA fire from the Kentish side of the river, along with the impending arrival of No. 61 Squadron's Pups, led Walter to direct his squadron home. One of the Gothas was destroyed over the sea (with the loss of the crew of *Leutnant* Hans Rolin, *Unteroffizier* Otto Rosinsky and *Unteroffizier* Rudi Stolle) and four were wrecked after crashing on landing, with at least one of the crew perishing.

The Eighth Gotha Daylight Raid

Saturday, 18 August 1917 (06.30-11.30) attack aborted before Harwich was reached.
28 planes (none crossed the English coast), 1 lost over the sea, 1 in Belgium, 2 in

Holland; around 9 were wrecked or damaged in landing crashes.

Kleine sanctioned the raid despite bad weather warnings and made for the nearest point of the English mainland, the North Foreland. In bright weather 28 bombers set out; however, strong winds blew them into neutral Holland and they suffered bombardment from AA guns, though none were hit. They managed to reach the open sea, but then met dense cloud cover and ended up off course heading for Harwich rather than the North Kent coast. With petrol supplies dwindling because of heavy headway and drifting, it was decided to abandon the raid and make for home, but one of the planes had to ditch in the sea when its fuel ran out. Another managed to glide to Zeebrugge, while two crash-landed in Holland and the crews were arrested. The Dutch also claimed they had shot at another Gotha and it had gone down in Belgium. Five more of the planes were downed by lack of fuel while four others were wrecked while trying to land, with *Leutnant* Adolf Hochgrabe killed. All in all it had been a disastrous sortie for the Germans, with almost half of the squadron wrecked in what had been an abandoned raid.

The Ninth Gotha Daylight Raid

Wednesday, 22 August 1917 (09.00-12.30) on Margate, Ramsgate and Dover.
15 planes (10 crossed the English coast), 50 bombs; casualties: 8 civilians killed, 12 injured (1 by AA fire); 4 military killed, 14 injured.
3 Gothas were shot down by AA fire and home aircraft.

The original target of the raid was London, but the squadron, now boasting some Gotha GVs, suffered an early setback when five of the planes suffered engine trouble, including Kleine's own craft. Approaching Margate the Gothas were met by RNAS aircraft from Manston, Eastchurch, Walmer and Dover and a barrage of effective AA fire. Two of the Gothas were downed, one by anti-aircraft fire and the other by Flight Sub-Lieutenant J Drake of 46 Squadron in a Sopwith Pup. One crashed at the top of Bird's Avenue, Garlinge, near Hengrove Golf Links, and its three crew of Heinrich Schildt, Eckart Fulda and *Vizefeldwebel* Eichelkamp all perished. The second Gotha landed in the sea at Walpole Bay, Margate: Werner Joschkowitz and Walter Latowski were killed, but Bruno Schneider survived and was rescued by HMS *Kestrel*. The five bombs that fell on Margate damaged houses in Windsor Avenue, Cliftonville Avenue, St Mildred's Road and the approach road, but caused no casualties.

The Gotha raid of 22 August 1917 accounted for this demolished house in Windsor Avenue, Cliftonville. Marlinova Collection

In the face of this effective home defence, Kleine's deputy Walter abandoned all hopes of attacking London and instead turned south for Dover. As the remaining eight planes flew over Ramsgate they dropped twenty-eight bombs on the town. One landed outside a store in Military Road and killed six men – John Debling (44), Henry Minter (63), Alfred Coomber (63), George Baker (71), Walter Spain (57) and Walter Melhuish (45) – who were sheltering there. Little Nellie Fittall (or Fox), aged 5 $^1/_2$, was critically injured and later died in hospital, and draper J Wright and three children were injured in Picton Road. At the Chatham House Canadian Army Hospital many patients had vacated the recreation room to view the burning Gotha over Margate just minutes before a bomb fell through the building. It descended through the chapel, dormitory and recreation room before exploding in the basement, killing staff butcher D R Creighton and injuring several men. Another bomb demolished Townley Castle, an annexe of Chatham House, used to house seriously disabled men. A Canadian soldier of the 5 Brigade Field Artillery, John Paul, was killed when a bomb landed on Church Hill, outside the *Thanet Observer* offices, and the decision was taken to move the Canadian

Behold the end of a raiding." Gotha,"
A prey to Kentish fire.
Our boys at the guns have finished the Hun
And lit their funeral pyre.

A Stirring Episode in the Raid of 22nd Aug., 1917.

The end for a Gotha shot down over Margate during the final daylight raid of 22 August 1917. Marlinova Collection

hospitals at Ramsgate and Broadstairs to a safer location. The library, Ramsgate County Schools, St Lawrence College and Ramsgate Town Station were all damaged in the raid, which was keenly observed in both Margate and Ramsgate by a Mrs Peile in her diary:

Wed. Aug 22nd – I had quite hoped we should get away from Margate without any further incident, but no such luck. Eric was to have arrived yesterday but never turned up and I am expecting him tonight. We had an awful air raid again this morning. To begin with I didn't sleep well last night owing to some heavy firing a long way off which kept rattling the doors and windows. Misomé and I started out early to do our shopping. The last shop I went to was Bobby's – I had just left it and was wheeling Misomé towards home when we saw a lot of people gazing skywards. On looking up too, we saw 3 or 4 aeroplanes a good height up and we were all very suspicious of them. At that moment I heard a funny sort of noise and I said to myself 'that's the Queens Hotel siren trying to start off' and in a few seconds it blazed forth.

Everyone started going for shelter and I decided to run back to Bobby's, as it was nearer than going home. Another spinal chair with a man in it was just going in and so we slipped in after him, chair as well. Mr Bobby called out to people in the streets to come inside quickly if they wanted to, as he had to lock the doors. Misomé got out of her chair, and we went down below where all the employees were sent. We knew a lot of the latter and they were so kind and nice to M. We had a box to sit on – all was quiet at first, but after about ten minutes, viz at 10.25 a.m. the first guns began and so we knew we were in for it. One or two of the employees were awfully frightened and began to weep etc and I was so afraid they would make M frightened too. As usual though she kept quite calm, but I could see she was nervous and I would be thankful to get her away. The guns made a fearful noise but we could hear the hum of many aeroplanes. Then we heard the first bomb, fairly near, and then came a terrible whistling through the air, and we realised that an aerial torpedo was coming down and it sounded so near that we guessed it would fall unpleasantly close. A lot of the employees made a dash for an inner doorway and then came the crash and we breathed once more. Several more bombs were dropped quite near, and then came a mighty cheer from some soldiers outside and a lot of the girls, heedless of flying bits of shell, tore up the iron staircase and then we heard them cheering too. They returned a few seconds later and said they had seen three aeroplanes falling down, two of them in flames. We all cheered too and it bucked us up. The firing still went on, and when at last it ceased it had been going on for 25 minutes. We did not get up for some time, but eventually we departed for home although the 'all clear' had not gone. Certainly Bobby's people had been extremely kind – Miss Rustall and Miss Potter had gone all right, but the former was very frightened. Several holes had been made in roofs in this raid and a large hole in the gutter from a shell. We hurried down to the front as we heard that a destroyer was just rescuing the Germans and the crew of one of our aeroplanes that had come down in the sea, but we only arrived in time to see the destroyer departing. Then we went to see the rest of the damage, fortunately no one was killed here. Three of the bombs and an aerial torpedo fell in the road where we were sheltering, viz Cliftonville Avenue, but the worst damage was in Windsor Avenue, where one house was completely destroyed and half of the next one to it. Fortunately the owner was out. I met her a little later, a Mrs Tatton, and she told me she had a sort of premonition that something would happen and had gone down early to the sands.

This evening went to Ramsgate with Mrs King Hall – three people were killed on the front and a sailor was blown off his ship but not killed. The worst damage was at Chatham Hospital – one bomb fell through a ward, injuring several of the patients but did not kill them as it only exploded when it reached the basement, where it killed the butcher. Such a nice, wounded Canadian soldier showed us the damage. He took us into the garden and showed us a shed, which had been completely destroyed, and where several patients had been badly injured, I do feel so sad for them. The station was also hit, apparently about ten German machines came over here. Tonight there is the most vivid summer lightning that I have ever seen; it was in the Ramsgate direction and Miss Rustall thought something else was happening and was very nervous. We pray for a quiet night.

The wrecked Canadian hospital at Chatham House, Ramsgate, where one person was killed during the Gotha raid on Ramsgate of 22 August 1917. Marlinova Collection

Upon the planes reaching Dover, nine bombs were dropped, killing two military personnel of the 32nd Training Reserve at Dover College and 17-year-old barmaid Lucy Wall at the Admiral Harvey pub. One bomb fell through the home of Mr and Mrs Hebden Phillips in Folkestone Road, but failed to explode. A third Gotha was downed off Dover, but the remaining seven aircraft managed to limp to Belgium, though five of the supporting squadron were lost. Seven Gotha crewmen were lost in the raid; those at Margate were buried in the town's cemetery. The wreckage of their aircraft was sold by auction for war charities at Margate Town Hall by the Mayor W B Reeve.

The daylight raids were then abandoned owing to the ever-increasing effectiveness of the home defences and the subsequent loss of Gothas. A total of 648 bombs had been dropped during the nine daylight raids, killing 400 and injuring almost 1,000 (compared to 1,414 killed and 3,416 wounded overall by German raids throughout the war). Thirty-two of the Gothas had been lost and fifty-seven of their crew were killed. While the bravery of the Gotha IV crews was undeniable, the plane itself proved to be in some cases rather shoddily built, under-powered with an unreliable engine, erratic in bad weather conditions and difficult to land, and its bombs were often defective. Yet the raids did achieve some success, particularly the 13 June sortie on London, while on the British side the disunity of the RNAS and RFC eventually led to the formation of the Royal Air Force in April 1918.

Kampfstaffel 13 (Squadron 13 of KAGOHL III) in the summer of 1917. Standing from left to right are Braun, unknown, Winsloe, Zahntier, Fiebig (Staffelführer – Squadron Leader), Schulte, Helbing, Scharffenberg, Radke, Schweider. Sitting left to right are Stöhr (Technischeroffizier – Technical Officer), Raulfs, Alex, Genth. Thomas Genth

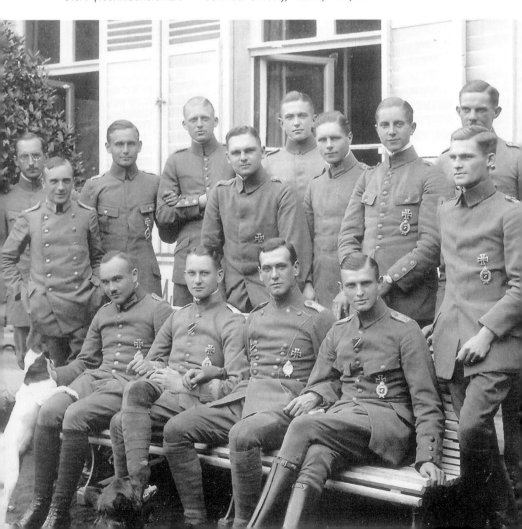

Chapter Twelve

MOONLIGHT MARAUDERS

GERMAN AIR AND SEA RAIDS,
SEPTEMBER 1917 TO AUGUST 1918

The Gothas were far from finished, and in September 1917 they were switched to night-time, or 'moonlight' raids. They were usually accompanied by the huge Staaken R-type aircraft, known as the 'Giant', which was twice the size of the Gothas.

The Giant was developed as a long-range aircraft by a corporation headed by Graf Ferdinand von Zeppelin. They formed the Versuchsbau GmbH Gotha-Ost (Experimental Works Gotha-East) and construction started in September 1914, with the first prototype taking to the air in April 1915. The factory was relocated to Staaken, near Berlin in 1916 and the production version, known as the Zeppelin Staaken Riesenflugzeug (giant aircraft), was produced for two army R-plane squadrons Rfa 500 and 501, initially based on the Eastern Front. The Giant was

Zeppelin Staaken RVI, the Riesenflugzeug, or R-type, known as the 'Giant'.
Thomas Genth

An R-type Giant with some of the crew members. Thomas Genth

technically well ahead of its time with its huge wingspan of 138 $^1/_2$ feet (the Lancaster bomber of the Second World War in comparison had a span of only 102 feet) and four 260hp Mercedes or Maybach engines. It could reach a maximum speed of 85mph and carry a bomb load of 220lb. Though the Staaken version of the R-plane was the one used on the raids against England, Siemens-Schuckert, DFW and AEG produced other versions of the aircraft. However, only around 300 of them were to reach the front line during the war.

In August 1917 Rfa 501 and its six planes was transferred to Belgium and placed under the operational control of KAGOHL III. On 28 September 1917 the first Giant, R39, was used on a bombing raid over England. This particular aircraft was to become the bombing champion of the squadron with 20 raids on English and French cities, dropping 26,000kg in bombs. In fact, the Giants were to have the perfect survival record over England with not one being lost throughout the bombing campaign.

The first of the moonlight raids was carried out against Dover on 2/3 September 1917, though only on a modest scale, by KAGOHL IV. At 11.30 pm in brilliant moonlight two machines dropped 14 bombs on the town in two minutes, causing a fair amount of damage. One of the bombs fell at the rear of Maison Dieu Road Post Office and shattered all the windows in the area. A Mrs Sergeant was blown bodily out of No. 6 Prospect Cottage and a Mrs Knight was also injured. Three bombs fell around Leyburne Road, wrecking the attic of No 17, and at 18 Castlemount Cottages young Daisy Warman suffered injuries. Crundall's sawmill had its roof blown off, while a bomb that landed in the garden of the Angel Inn blew out windows in the High Street and Wood Street. The only fatality from the raid was caused by the three bombs that fell on the Northfall Meadow army camp; Second Lieutenant Larcombe of the 5th Battalion, Royal Fusiliers, being the unlucky victim. An officer and three men of the same regiment were injured.

The people of Dover were soon to become used to these raids over the coming year and learnt to take shelter in caverns under the Western Heights, in the crypt of the Town Hall and the cellar of the Phoenix Brewery.

On the following night, five Gothas set out on KAGOHL III's first night attack, though one had to turn back over the Channel with engine trouble. Poor Margate, which had very little significant military value was targeted again (perhaps one of the Gotha commanders had spent a bad holiday there before the war!) According to the clock that was later found shattered on Marine Parade, the raid had commenced by 11.12 pm, but caused little damage, as did the bombs that landed on neighbouring St Peters and Northdown. The Gothas then set off for the naval dockyard towns of Sheerness and Chatham; the latter proving to be a particularly enticing target owing to the fact a telephone call to the power station to extinguish all lights was not taken seriously. For the naval ratings sleeping peacefully in their hammocks in the drill hall at Chatham Naval Barracks the results were

The drill shed at the Royal Naval Barracks Chatham, pictured shortly before the war. In 1917 it was being used as sleeping quarters and during a moonlight raid on 3/4 September 1917 a bomb fell through the glass roof, mortally wounding 132 naval ratings sleeping in their hammocks. Marlinova Collection

devastating. One bomb fell clean through the building with horrific consequences as flying splinters from the shattered glass roof cut to pieces 132 men (some sources claim 136), the highest death-toll from one single bomb dropped on home soil during the war. In addition 90 men were severely injured. The hall had been requisitioned as a sleeping dormitory because of an outbreak of spotted fever (cerebro-spinal meningitis) in the barracks.

E Cronk was at the naval barracks on that fateful night and vividly remembered the carnage:

> The raider dropped two bombs, one in the middle of the drill shed and one near the wall of the parade ground just where the sailors were sleeping. I shall never forget that night – the lights fading and the clock stopping at 11.10 p.m., we of the rescue party picking out bodies, and parts of bodies, from among glass and debris and placing them in bags, fetching out bodies in hammocks and laying them on a tarpaulin on the parade ground (you could not identify them). I carried one sailor to the sick bay who was riddled with shrapnel and had no clothes left on him. In the morning, to show that the officials could tell who was who, they had a General Pipe asking all sailors of different messes if they could identify any of the lost; it was impossible in most cases. It was one of the most terrible nights I have ever known – the crying and moaning of dying men who had ten minutes before been fast asleep.

The *Chatham News* further added:

> All through the night the work of rescue went on. It was a sad spectacle in the moonlight – officers and men carrying the dead bodies of comrades into buildings, which had been transformed into a mortuary and the seriously wounded cases into motor ambulances, which sped to the hospital.

The Brompton area of Gillingham close to the dockyard was hit by a number of

The wreckage of a house in Surrey Road, Cliftonville, hit during the Gotha attack of 4/5 September 1917. Marlinova Collection

bombs. A sailor was killed in Maxwell Road and his friend and their two girlfriends were injured. Brompton School was damaged, and in May Road the roof of one house was left with a splattered patch of white and yellow liquid, which due to the terrific stench was probably a poison or noxious gas. In addition, houses in Marlborough Road, York Avenue, College Avenue and Mansion Row suffered structural damage.

In Chatham one civilian was killed when houses in Church Terrace were destroyed. The High Street, Trinity School and the Lines also suffered destruction from the German bombs.

The Gothas returned in force the following night, 4/5 September 1917, when 26 planes attacked London and the Home Counties, causing 19 deaths and 71 wounded. Margate was once again a target and 8 people were injured in Cliftonville. Around 40 properties were damaged, including some in Eastern Esplanade and Cornwall Gardens, and 13 Surrey Road was completely demolished. A courting couple walking along Surrey Road were injured outside the Hotel Florence. However, one of the Gothas was shot down, with *Unteroffizier* Theodor Fries known to have perished.

Dover was also attacked that night, from around 10.30 pm. Two 200lb trench mortar shells, known as 'Crashing Christophers', landed on Priory Hill and although neither exploded, H Long was killed when one of the shells fell through his house. Two further fatalities occurred when a huge bomb wrecked Nos. 4 and 6 Widred Road. Edward Little (73) was killed at No. 4 and Mrs Minnie Smith never recovered from her injuries. Her husband suffered a broken leg, and also wounded were Mrs Voller and her son and Mrs Holland. Damage to property in the town was pretty widespread. A line of bombs was dropped from Pencester Meadow to the Corporation dust dump at Union Road, where No. 56 was wrecked. At nearby Odo Road No. 14 was severely damaged, Tolputt's timber yard was hit again and properties in Queens Court were shattered by a bomb that fell at the back of Meadows' in the High Street. After the raid further air-raid shelters were commissioned in the town, including the Oil Mill Caves.

Twenty days later they were put to the test when, on 24/25 September 1917, 21 aircraft of KG3 attacked London, Essex and Kent killing 21 (including 14 in London and 6 in Dover) and wounding 70 (12 in Dover). The squadron attacked Dover at around midnight, with some of the first bombs seemingly aimed for the Priory Station. The Wesley Hall in Folkestone Road was wrecked and another bomb landed in the garden of 10 Folkestone Road, where a Miss Pilcher was conducting a shorthand class with six girls present (at midnight!) All seven ladies were injured and Miss Dorothy Wood later died. No. 55 Folkestone Road was also wrecked, as was 3 Selbourne Terrace. The back of 40 Glenfield Road, adjoining the Dover-Deal railway, was blown in and Mrs Annie Keats was immediately killed, with her daughter Evelyn later dying in hospital. The planes followed the line of the railway and another bomb flattened two houses in Pioneer Road. No. 75 Crabble Hill was also wrecked, burying the unfortunate Miss Ellen Kenward under a pile of rubble; her lifeless body eventually being extricated in the dark of night by soldiers of the Works Corps. Miss Kenward, whose father Edward later died of his injuries, had been on her way to assist the bedridden Miss Gould next door, who also later died in hospital, of shock. The Germans eventually managed to hit the railway, and the

The air-raid refuge at Oil Mills Cave, Dover. Marlinova Collection

gasworks also suffered, while another bomb that fell on Baldock's traction-engine works caused considerable damage to properties in the immediate area. During the 20-minute raid, 48 bombs were dropped on the town, and although Sheppey, Chatham and West Malling were also targeted, but little damage was caused.

The Prime Minister, David Lloyd George, was in Dover while the raid was in progress and subsequently ordered the barrage defences to be strengthened. Yet the raid had left the people of Dover helpless and disturbed at the inefficiency of the defensive measures. On the following night some of them camped out at the nearby villages of River, Temple Ewell and West Hougham, where they felt safer. Dover was visited again that night, but this time the enemy was beaten off by a tremendous barrage and no bombs were dropped. Thanet also received a visit from the bombers but the only casualty was a horse at Northdown. However, in south-east London, nine people were killed and twenty-three wounded. Two of the Gothas were downed, with *Flugmeister* Hermann Mochatzky, *Leutnant* Hermann von Scharfenort, *Leutnant* Alfred Herzberg and *Leutnant* Franz Rahning listed as casualties.

A further Gotha (with *Vizefeldwebel* Heinrich Schreiber and *Leutnant* Martin Emmler listed as lost) was downed during the raid of 28/29 September 1917 in which twenty-five Gothas and two Giants took part (although only three Gothas dropped their bombs). Another was lost off the Dutch coast and a third was reputed to have crashed. Dover and Minster were attacked without casualties, but in Deal Mrs Edith Owers, a widow residing at Verrier's Cottages, Middle Deal Road, suffered fatal injuries when an anti-aircraft shell burst on impact outside her cottage. *Oberleutnant* Fritz Lorenz was one of the Germans who took part in this raid and left his impressions of a night attack in the book *Unsere Luftstreitkräfte 1914/1918*:

BOGOHL III attacked the British Isles for the first time at the 25th of May 1917 in bright daylight and brought the fright of the war far away from the battle fields to the nerve center of our strongest enemy. They repeated these attacks with all their energy but were forced because of the growing losses during the summer months, to change to night attacks.

For the attacks against England exact maps had been given to the crews, showing the high priority military targets, which our bombers should hit, and only those were our targets.

The growing power of the anti aircraft guns and fighters, but also the less and less powerful possibilities of our own aircraft forced us to fly at night. The reached climb rates of our twin engine Gothas became worse and worse and were finally so bad, that it was impossible to fly a successful attack during daylight. The 22nd of August 1917 was the last day we were able to see the British Isles in bright daylight lying under us.

In spite of the crews of the squadron not being really prepared for the night flights, they faced it optimistically and with much energy.

During the night of the 3rd to 4th September 1917 the Gothas bombed military targets at the coastal towns of Chatham, Sheerness and Margate and in the following night, they reached London, bombing the targeted military installations for about one and a half hour.

The demoralizing effect of these night attacks against the British capital, in which thousands of inhabitants were forced to flee into the subways, must have been very strong during the 24th of September and 2nd of October 1917; in this period London had to face six 'Gotha alarms'.

It was one of these nights, exactly the 28th/29th of September, which is still in my mind. For the third time since the 24th of September, we were preparing for take off against London. 'We'- means my skillful 'Emil' (the nickname for the pilot in WW1), Leutnant *Kurt Kueppers*, an old pilot from the time before of the war, and me, the "Franz" (nickname for the observer in WW1). For being able to carry more bomb load, we normally refused to take a rear gunner with us and also had no machine guns at the rear positions.

In spite of being targeted a lot of times by some English fighters at night, which found us because of our glowing exhaust pipes, I never managed it to locate these fighters absolutely for sure, so that I never could respond to the fire in a way that would give me some success.

But this special night, we had a third man on board, Hauptmann Muehlich-Hoffmann, who accidentally found our airfield Gontrode coming from the headquarters, to get information about the squadron's demands. He wanted to get a picture himself of what we were doing and obtained the allowance to accompany us this night. So he became our rear gunner for this flight.

When we drove out to the airfield, it started to grow dark. From the west there were some thin clouds moving in, but they couldn't influence the bright moonlight very much. The weather forecast said that the clouds should become thicker, but they shouldn't reach more than 300 metres thickness, and so we decided to take off.

With the last twilight the aircraft left the ground of the airfield. We flew the well-known way to Ostend. The thin clouds didn't affect us much at the moment, but towards the sea it looked as if they were getting bigger and bigger. When we reached the open sea, it was night. We were flying over a milky white ocean of clouds, above which the full moon was shining in an inhospitable bright light. A wonderful clear firmament leads us – beside the compass – on the way. We at the squadron had learnt the experience that the Arcturus, a bright star, gave for the airplanes that took off at the early evening, a good direction towards London. The star was soon called 'Sturius' according to the humor of our comrade v. der Nahmer ['stur' in German means somebody who is not looking right or left – just straight] who would soon be killed at the side of our knightly commander Hauptmann Kleine, because you only had to head for it to reach London, if the wind had no further surprises for the crew. He even constructed the "Sturometer", a big fork, located at the front machine gun ring, so that the pilot could find the direction to London by keeping the 'Sturius' in that fork.

Also this night the 'Sturius' showed us the way, but we didn't need it really this time, there were exploding grenades in front of us. The enemy anti aircraft fire could be seen from Dover to the Thames River, and like through a milky glass there were spots to be seen, which were searching the clouds. Yet only a few times could they penetrate the cloud layer and they will hardly catch the comrades in front of us.

When we approached the English coastline, it was getting more and more calm. The anti aircraft guns could only be heard from time to time, perhaps they had to stop due to the growing clouds. In a fruitless search, the reflectors were painting big white plates into the ocean of clouds under us. Where normally a hell of exploding grenades blocked the way for every airplane, today there was only a peaceful kind of loneliness. Ghostly the moonlight was drawing our shadow at the white blanket under us. The minutes passed. Holes in the clouds became less and less; it was impossible to navigate by landmarks. Also the River Thames was unable to be located in the picture of clouds, where sometimes bigger rivers could be seen by the different shape of the clouds. So we were limited by stars, compass and clock. No enemy bullet was fired against us the whole long way, so we thought of ourselves maybe as ghosts. Was it possible, that a few nights ago at the same location, there had been a wall of iron, steel and fire? To imagine the waste of power of the English anti aircraft guns is to imagine the fact that these guns fired more ammunition in one night, than the both sides of the Front on a big fighting day in Flanders did.

But today it was dismal calm. Finally after a flight time of exactly two hours twenty minutes, the English capital betrayed itself by the play of the numerous reflectors giving a shine to the clouds in a wide area. Sometimes – for a fragment of a second through a hole in the clouds, there were streets of lights to be seen under us, the streets of a big city.

We reached our target, which we wouldn't have found so easily without the betrayal of the reflectors. A few levers were pulled, a light vibration shook the aircraft and the torpedo-like 50 and 100kg bombs were searching their way through the clouds, soundless – bringing destruction to the ones on the ground.

Now we were heading back home, right the way along the River Thames, which *we couldn't see of course. Orientation was done only with the compass, while the 'Sturius' behind us, after finishing his job, came down to the westerly horizon to rest. The clouds under us were forming a huge light ocean, above which we were flying in an altitude of nearly 4,000 metres. The two brave engines were singing their song, pulling us home with their power of 480hp. The beauty of the fairytale-like moon above the ocean of boiling milk-like clouds, the glitter of the stars, the endless loneliness – I never forgot this picture and often it comes back to me in my dreams until today.*

Very soon though, we had to face the fact that we needed to go down through the cloud layer. It had to happen before reaching the Flandric coastline, because we needed to find landmarks in the dark telling us where we were and to show the further way back to the airfield. On my order, Küppers started the descent. We were dipping into the white foam, after a few seconds it became completely dark, indescribably oppressing – we could hardly breathe. It was nearly impossible to watch the instruments a few centimetres away through the wet fog. We were still descending, more and more down. The altimeter showed 2,500m, then 2,000, 1,500 – then reached 1,000m. The darkness would not end. We were condemned to a crushing weakness. The struts and the control wires were clattering because of our dive; the compass started to spin with growing speed. Finally we were no longer flying but in a spin. The pilot's sense of balance – and he was one of the most experienced – began to fail. Also here the strange experience was proved, that the non-piloting passenger in fog and clouds keeps his sense of balance longer than the pilot. As good as I could, I tried to show Küppers with my arms the horizontal plane, at the same time I was looking out desperately to find a fixed point outside, some sign, that we were through this terrible darkness. In vain!

The spiral dive got narrow and narrower. With a clattering noise, the right strut broke and fluttered like a dismal pennant at the upper wing. 800m – 500m – 300m – finally 100m could be seen on the altimeter. It was like a ring of iron pressed my chest. My teeth were gnashing in a fainting rage. God, there had to be an end of this terrible darkness! My eyes were staring to the ground, until it physically hurt. The needle showed only 50 metres – then, finally under us a nearly invisible gleam, the waves of the sea, so close we thought we could touch them. It was the absolutely last second which we had to use. How Küppers did it – nobody on board remembered – enough – my brave Küppers got the aircraft under control again, we were still flying. Now we were out of the haze, but the darkness above the water was dismal, especially when we thought about the wonderful light above the clouds, which were blocking all this light for us flying under them. Very near under us, there was the boiling sea; we had no idea where to fly to reach the coastline. Where was the coastline? The compasses refused to give an answer. They were spinning around in their housings and all the tricks we learned to make them work didn't help. I cancelled my efforts to bring the front compass back to work and crept to the pilot's seat; maybe I would be more successful here. After a while I noticed a little success. When I let the rear compass fall back into his mount, he finally offered me only two directions. After repeating this several times, there was a little plus for one direction, which I believed must be north. If I was right, we should reach the Flandric coastline soon – if not a wet grave would be waiting for us. So the minutes passed, the heavy burden, the feeling of responsibility for the whole crew in this unsafe situation was still in my mind. The futility of all human knowledge in a fight against the elementary power of nature became painfully clear to me.

Then suddenly – there was a near and clearly visible intermittent light above the waves. Long – short, short – long – short – short. Ostend! From one moment to the other I felt like tons of burdens were taken away from me. The way back home was in reach. With some more hard work, we found our way through the dark night in low level and landed safely at our airfield, four hours and 45 minutes after leaving it for England.

The squadron believed that we didn't make it this time, in this night only one other aircraft reached London and made – after the attack – a crash landing at the coastline. The night took from the squadron some crews and many aircraft, but the crews lost always showed a lot of nerve.

'Iron and crazy', that was our motto, which was painted in big letters at the wings of our aircraft. So the next night saw us again on our way towards London. This time it was much more hectic, but we both loved it more this way ... .

On the following night (29/30 September 1917) a raid by seven Gothas and three Giants killed 14 and injured 87, mostly in London, though one Gotha was brought down off Dover by a gun barrage. Sheerness and its surrounding district were unsuccessfully attacked, and four bombs aimed at the explosive works on Faversham Creek missed.

There was no respite as the Gothas kept on coming. On the night of 30 September/1 October 1917, London, Chatham, Margate, Broadstairs and Dover were all attacked. Margate came off worst, suffering 11 of the 14 fatalities, and altogether there were 38 wounded. Five of the casualties were military personnel; three of them – John Gratty, Thomas Armstrong and Frank Williams – serving in the Canadian Army attached to the Royal Engineers at Sandwich. The three sappers, who were killed when a bomb exploded in Cliff Terrace, were probably working on the secret Richborough Port, where materials were shipped to the Western Front. Though serving with the Canadians, the three men were actually British and had all enlisted together in New York as they were living in the USA when the war began. The three pals were rightly laid to rest together, in Margate Cemetery.

During the raid 13 HE and 13 incendiary bombs were dropped on Margate. Cliff Terrace was also where 40-year-old Jane Lee met her death, at No. 10, and in St Paul's Road Private Benjamin Farnhill of the 18th Battalion, Yorkshire Regiment was killed by shrapnel whilst sheltering in a doorway. One of the bombs fell on the pavement in front of the greengrocer's shop at 82 Trinity Square and killed the owner, Mrs Eliza Emptage, and Private William Hollins, a driver in the 834th Company, Army Service Corps, who was standing by the door. The whole building collapsed into the street and Mr and Mrs Thomas Parker (both aged 62) later succumbed to their injuries, though Mrs Emptage's mother was recovered from the wreckage suffering only two broken legs. The other two civilian fatalities were Mrs Alice Coleman at 36 Buckingham Road and 47-year-old William Walker, who died in hospital after suffering injuries in Milton Road. Three of the bombs landed in Dane Park, and other roads to be affected included Sweyn Road, Godwin Road, Ethelbert Terrace, Alexandra Road, Helena Avenue, Marlborough Road and Buckingham Road.

Neighbouring Broadstairs escaped lightly, with little damage suffered from bombs falling at Elmwood Farm, Reading Street and St Percy Avenue, Kingsgate (where an unexploded bomb landed on a bed). Dover was also lightly treated, with just three bombs falling on the town proper, at an engineering works in Bridge Street, at No. 59 Peter Street (where shrapnel injured H Marshall of No. 35) and amongst allotments in Castle Avenue.

Margate was also attacked the following evening (1/2 October 1917), but this time suffered no casualties, although the Victoria Convalescent Home in Stone Road was set alight and the gasworks, cottage hospital, Wesleyan Church and the Liberal Club were all damaged.

On the night of 19 October 1917 a fleet of 11 Zeppelins came over in what became known as the 'Silent Raid' in a bid to restore their influence. They floated all over the country, but concentrated on large cities such as Sheffield, Manchester and Liverpool. One of the airships, L49, with *Kapitänleutnant* Hans Gayer commanding, flew over the Folkestone area on its return and was fired on by anti-aircraft batteries at Shorncliffe and Lympne. Despite inflicting 36 deaths and some 55 wounded, the fragility of the airships was fully exposed once again when five of them were downed (including an intact L49); four in France and one in Germany, due to a combination of Allied aircraft and strong winds.

The Gothas were a much less visible target, however, and continued to come over in waves. On 31 October/1 November 1917 both London and a large area of Kent were attacked, leaving 10 dead and 22 wounded. One of the fatalities occurred in Gillingham when a Mr Tapsell was killed in his bed in Canterbury

Gotha GIV (LVG) 991/16 crashed into a Belgian farmhouse on 11 November 1917. MOROTAS stands for Leutnant Mons, Leutnant Roland and possibly Unteroffizier Hermann Tasche. Thomas Genth

Street by an unexploded anti-aircraft shell, which also wrecked Moakes's Bakery, hurling bread, cakes and bags of flour out into the street. Both Byron Road and Barnsole Road infants' schools had their windows blown out, as did the backs of houses in Pretoria Road. Chatham Dockyard was also hit and a Royal Marine was reported to have been killed. Nearby Gravesend was also attacked, with Prospect Place being the worst-affected area.

Thanet was also given its usual dousing, with bombs falling on Margate, Ramsgate, Kingsgate, Northdown and Garlinge, though to little effect. However, the gasworks at Ramsgate suffered extensive damage, as did Aberdeen House School in South Eastern Road. In Margate, three weeks after the raid an unexploded bomb was found in the kitchen of a house in Windsor Avenue.

Dover was reached at 10.30 pm and 22 incendiary bombs were unloaded on the harbour and foreshore, causing fires at the seaplane base and on board the cross-Channel boat *Princess Victoria*. One large HE bomb fell close to the Prince of Wales Pier; killing a seaman sheltering under the pier and wounding his companion, and the well-known officer, Lieutenant Godfrey RNR, died from a heart attack during the raid.

Kent was next attacked, along with London and Essex, on 5/6 December 1917 and suffered five out of the eight fatalities from the raid. Sheerness was worst affected, with three civilians and a sailor killed when bombs fell on the Invicta Road area. In No. 141, Mary Anne Hubbard (55), her son James (31) and his wife Rosa and their seven-year-old daughter were all asleep when a bomb landed on the house. Rosa and the little girl managed to escape relatively unscathed, but both Mary Ann and James were killed. Another house struck was 129 Invicta Road, causing the death of Louisa Cox (37), though her husband and children sleeping in the same room only suffered minor injuries. Nearby, Horace Mouatt, a 27-year-old naval shipwright aboard HMS *Actaeon*, who had served at the Battle of Jutland, was killed when falling masonry fractured his skull.

In Margate Mrs A Roberts was killed in the house adjoining the Oxford pub in Oxford Street. A further person was injured by the 30 bombs dropped on the town in Broad Street, Oxford Street, High Street, Norfolk Road, Byron Road, Devonshire Gardens, Buckingham Road, Park Crescent and Hartsdown Road. Whitstable and Dover were also attacked, but with little effect, although in Dover a paint store was set alight on the floating dock and a quantity of hand grenades were blown up at Connaught Barracks. Yet the county had the satisfaction of seeing one of the three Gothas downed that night crash-land at Folly Farm, St Stephen's, adjacent to Broad Oak Road, Canterbury. First on the scene was a Red Cross orderly, Mr J B Wilford of Mandeville Road, Canterbury, who, noticing that two of the three crew were injured, offered assistance. However, one of the crew held Mr Wilford at gunpoint while a comrade set the plane alight, but the Germans surrendered after the Revd Philip Somerville (a special constable) and G W Haines arrived on the scene. The injured crew were taken to hospital, where they were kindly treated, and very thankful for the hospitality. The Gotha crew were named as *Leutnant* S R Schulte, *Vizefeldwebel* B Senf and gunner *Leutnant* P W Bernard. The burnt-out Gotha proved to be a great object of curiosity for thousands of people, who on viewing the plane donated £32 to the Red Cross.

Two further Gothas were to be brought down over Kent during raids on 18/19 and 22/23 December 1917. Twenty Gothas, now led by Richard Walter owing to the death of Kleine on 12 December, headed the raid of the 18th and Margate was once more selected as a secondary target. The town suffered three different attacks between 6.00 and 8.00 pm and 150 houses were damaged in Addington Road, Glencoe Road, Dane Road, Upper Grove, Clifton Terrace, Victoria Road and Carraways Place. Buildings damaged included the schoolroom of the Emmanuel Church, the Foresters' Hall and Clifton Baths, yet fortunately there was only one injury, to a Miss Clark, in her arm.

One of the Gothas was hit by guns at Westenhanger and came down in the sea 3 miles off Folkestone. The pilot, *Leutnant* Friedrich Ketelsen, was killed, but the two surviving crew were picked up by a trawler. Unfortunately the Gotha had a sting in its tail; it was blown up by a time-fused bomb, fatally injuring 47-year-old trawlerman Frank Gee, who was helping to bring it aboard. A second Gotha crashed in Belgium, killing *Leutnant* Otto Vüllers, *Leutnant* Hans Baasch and *Vizefeldwebel* Reinhold Nesemann. Four days later another Gotha crashed because of engine failure at Hartsdown Farm, Garlinge. The pilot, G Hoffmann, set fire to the machine and then surrendered, along with the navigator W Dobrick and gunner H Klaus, to Margate Police. Machine guns thrown overboard from the plane were found the next day at Grosvenor Place and Twenties Farm.

By 1918, the sustained night-time raids on London had led to 300,000 Londoners taking shelter in the tube stations. Sadly this was not enough to prevent 67 losing

The different bomb sizes, pictured in front of a Gotha GV. Thomas Genth

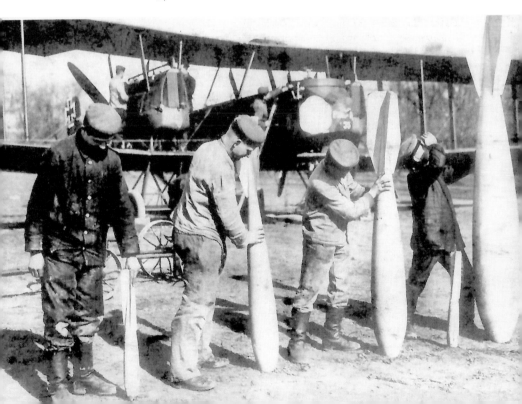

their lives and 166 being wounded during a raid by ten Gothas and three Giants on the night of 28/29 January 1918. Over half the casualties, 37 killed and 89 wounded, were caused by one 112lb bomb that fell on Messrs Oldham's printing works in Long Acre, which was being used as an air-raid shelter. Two military personnel were killed when Sheerness was targeted, one of them being Able Seaman A Winmill aboard HMS *Wildfire*. Seven aerial torpedoes were also unloaded on Ramsgate during the raid, damaging 100 houses. The Revd Thomas Hancock's house, at the corner of Crescent Road, had its back blown out, leaving the bathroom suspended in mid-air, and properties in South Eastern Road and Picton Road were also hit. Margate was the recipient of one bomb that fell on Laleham Road. Of the fifteen Gothas that set out, one was brought down in Essex and its three crew of *Unteroffizier* Wahlter Heiden, *Leutnant* Friedrich von Thomsen and *Unteroffizier* Karl Ziegler were killed.

However, the bravado was not confined to the German pilots, for on the night of 16/17 February 1918 the Imperial German Navy flexed its muscles and sent five destroyers to bombard Dover. The shelling began just after midnight and in four minutes 30 shots were fired at the town, 22 landing inside the borough. One hit the roof of Nos. 3 and 4 Cowgate Hill blowing down the wall between the two houses. Thirteen-year-old Gertrude Boorman was killed at No. 4 and her brothers Willie (15) and Sidney (9) and sister Amelia (11) were injured. Mr F C Shovelier sustained a slight injury in No. 3. A woman inmate suffered minor injuries when Dover Union Infirmary was hit, while two soldiers received wounds when a shell hit the old prison close to Langdon Battery. Houses in Maison Dieu Road, Dour Street, Peter Street, Devonshire Road, Harold Terrace, Westmount Road, Victoria Park and East Cliff all suffered damage.

Resistance to the raiders was pretty futile and much-criticized afterwards. The Dover Patrol had already suffered a bloody nose when eight of its craft had been sunk, while the Langdon AA battery had fired only one round in reply. The Battery Commander had been acting under orders not to fire on sea vessels without the authority of the Naval Commander in Chief, Admiral Bacon, because he contended they could not distinguish hostile from friendly vessels.

On the same evening Giant R25 dropped 23 bombs on St Margaret's-at-Cliffe. The Corner Cottage, the convent and houses belonging to H Hayward and Mr Elliff were all damaged, though no one was hurt. Another Giant, R33, had to prematurely drop its bombs into the sea off Deal because of engine failure and only just made it back to Belgium on one engine. London was also affected that night, with Giant R39 dropping the first 1,000kg bomb, which blew apart the North Pavilion of the Royal Hospital, Chelsea, killing the family of six of a Household Officer. Woolwich was also similarly affected with seven people killed by two 300kg bombs dropped by Giant R12.

The following night (17/18 February 1918) saw a further raid against the Dover area, when 20 bombs were unloaded, though again with little effect. Margate and Sheerness were targeted by three Giants on the evening of 7/8 March 1918 during a raid on London that saw a second 1,000kg bomb demolish 23 houses in Maida Vale, killing twelve. Four Giants set out for Dover on the night of 9/10 May 1918, but had to abort the raid due to bad weather, and French coastal towns were targeted instead.

Gotha pilots pose in front of a downed Handley Page 0/100 bomber. In the centre is Hauptmann Ernst Brandenburg and behind his right shoulder is Oberleutnant Aschoff, who wrote the book Londonflüge 1917. Behind Brandenburg's left shoulder is Adolf Genth. Thomas Genth

The last hurrah for the German air campaign against Britain occurred on the night of 19/20 May 1918. Thirty-eight Gothas, three Giants and two C-types set out for England carrying 14,550kg of HE bombs, including a 1,000-pounder, with thirty-four aircraft crossing the English coast for the largest assault of the war. Eighteen Gothas and one Giant reached London for a final onslaught on the capital of the British Empire, and in Kent, Dover, Faversham, Detling Aerodrome and Margate were all hit. Forty-nine people were killed (forty-eight in London) and 177 injured, yet the loss of ten of the Gothas and twenty-one of their crew signalled the end of the aircraft raids. Two of the downed Gothas crashed in Kent; one in flames at Harty on the Isle of Sheppey, killing its three crew of Rudolf Bartikowski (observer), Fritz Block (pilot) and Heinrich Hellgers (gunner). The other came down at Frinsted, where Joachim Flatlow (observer) and Albrecht Sachtler (pilot) were killed, but rear gunner Hermann Tasche survived. A further Gotha was brought down in the sea by the Langdon gun at Dover.

A total of forty-nine bombs were dropped on Kent during the raid, with Dover suffering the worst. Three bombs fell around the Priory Station area, two in Priory Hill Villas causing great damage to houses in the area and injuring a Miss Joad at No. 6, and the other in the station yard, which failed to explode. A fourth bomb landed in Widred Road, Tower Hamlets and decimated houses in the area. On the outskirts of Dover six bombs were dropped on Langdon Airfield, Guston and another six at St Margaret's-at-Cliffe, which landed harmlessly in wheat fields.

Margate's St Mary's Church suffered broken windows, but otherwise little damage was caused by bombs that fell on the sands and in the neighbouring areas of Northdown, St Nicholas-at-Wade and Acol. In Faversham, coal merchant Bill Norton was unfortunately blinded by a bomb that fell at the junction of Norman and Saxon Roads. However, the townsfolk rallied around him and a subscription fund was set up to make his life that little bit better. The two bombs that landed on Detling Aerodrome caused no damage whatsoever.

With the war now turning against Germany, the raids by BOGOHL III on England no longer had any propaganda or operational purpose and were halted, though there was still the odd scare. On 17 June 1918 an enemy bomber landed in a field near Foreness Point, Margate after getting lost in fog while bombing Ostend.

An unknown Gotha GV after a crash-landing on 23 May 1918. Notice the moon face on the nose. Thomas Genth

Hauptmann *Ernst Brandenburg, centre, poses for the last time with some of his officers at Frankfurt-an-der-Oder, where BOGOHL III was disbanded shortly after the armistice. On his right are Adolf Genth and Radke, and on his left Stöhr and Georgii of the headquarters staff.* Thomas Genth

The original military file of Adolf Genth. Column II lists some of his special flights during the war. These include the Folkestone raid, marked '25.5.1917 Geschwaderangriff auf Folkestone' (25 May 1917 squadron attack against Folkestone). Thomas Genth

The crew were on the verge of setting fire to their machine when they were apprehended. Just over a month later, on 28 July 1918, a solitary raider made a daring attempt to attack Ramsgate, but was soon beaten off.

The very last raid of the war occurred on 5/6 August 1918 when the head of the German Naval Airship Service, *Fregattenkapitän* Peter Strasser led an attack by five Zeppelins heading for East Anglia. At the head of the raid was L70 (LZ112), the most modern airship in the service, but led by the inexperienced *Kapitänleutnant* Johann von Lossnitzer. The raid was to go horribly wrong when, 8 miles off the coast, L70 was attacked by Major Edgar Cadbury and Robert Leckie in a DH4 and came down in flames, killing all 22 people on board including Strasser and von Lossnitzer and causing the raid to be aborted. An intended raid on the same day by planes equipped with the Elektron incendiary bomb was cancelled just half an hour before the off.

By this time the British were exacting some sort of revenge by carrying out air raids themselves on western Germany using their own giant, the Handley Page V/1500. By the war's end on 11 November 1918 these 'Bloody Paralysers', as they were dubbed, had killed 746 and injured 1,843.

In the same period the number of people killed in German air raids on Kent was 336, including 132 in Chatham Dockyard, 72 in Folkestone, 26 in Dover, 25 in Ramsgate, 18 in Margate, 18 at Shorncliffe Camp, 15 in Sheerness, 15 at Otherpool Camp, 3 in Broadstairs, 3 in Cheriton, 2 in Hythe, 2 in Chatham, 2 in Gillingham, 2 in Deal and Walmer, and 1 in Ashford.

Adolf Genth's medals from the First World War. The highest decoration, the Koeniglichen Hausorden der Hohenzollerscher mit Schwerfern *is in the centre; to the left is an Iron Cross first class. Adolf's skill and bravery led him to become Adjutant of BOGOHL III in 1918.*

Thomas Genth

Adolf's Observer's Badge from the First World War.

Thomas Genth

Chapter Thirteen

TIME, THE GREAT HEALER

THE PHYSICAL AND PERSONAL LEGACY OF THE RAIDS

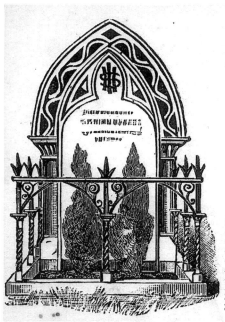

In Memory of
THE

MANY VICTIMS
OF THE

Aeroplane Raids
Over England.

By which large numbers of men, women and children have been killed and injured.

LIST OF AEROPLANE RAIDS.

			Killed		Injd.
May 25	Folkestone	.. .. ..	76	..	177
June 5	Medway	.. ..	12	..	36
June 13	London	.. ..	157	..	432
July 4	Harwich	.. .. ..	11	..	36
July 7	London & Isle of Thanet		43	..	197
July 23	Harwich and Felixstowe		11	..	26
Aug. 12	Southend	.. .. ..	32	..	43
Aug. 22	Dover	.. ..	11	..	26
Sept. 3	Chatham and Sheerness		120	..	70
Sept. 4	London and Chatham		11	..	62

A card produced just after the war listing the worst of the Gotha raids. The numbers killed and the places mentioned are not always strictly correct. Peter and Annie Bamford

Of all the Kentish towns affected by enemy action in the First World War, Ramsgate's scars were perhaps the most visible. Mrs A Purbrook visited 'the most bombed town in England' in 1918 and commented:

I can't say it was cheerful or uplifting. There are rows of empty houses, many with all the windows missing, burst by the concussion of bombing explosions. Constantly one came across the houses completely wrecked; there would be great gaps in the road, and one could not help imagining the terrors suffered by the poor people who

The spoils of war: UB21 tied up in Ramsgate Harbour. Marlinova Collection

inhabited them. Much damage had been done by a mine bursting in the harbour and by shelling from the sea. Altogether the people had a very bad time and appeared depressed and out of spirits. The house in which we stayed has twice had all the windows blown out and there was an underground refuge, which our landlady took us down to see. It was damp and uninviting; but I should think safe from Zeppelin bombs. Anchored in the sea were many trophies of war, vessels of many and various kinds taken from the Germans.

Gotha and Zeppelin trophies of the war may still be viewed in Kent today at Canterbury's Westgate Museum, Dover Museum, Hawkinge Battle of Britain Museum and RAF Manston History Museum.

Folkestone's heavy military presence dispersed and the soldiers' rest camps in the West End reverted to elegant hotels and superior residences as both residents and visitors began returning to the town. For those who were still mourning their loved ones, the offer to the town of a Gotha in February 1919 appeared to be nothing short of a sick joke. Not surprisingly the Council refused the offer, on the grounds they had no building in which to house the plane, but of course they were hardly likely to want to display the cause of the single biggest modern-day disaster to befall the civil population of Folkestone. Like many towns they acquired an Allied tank instead, which was placed on the Durlocks on 24 July 1919. Neighbouring Hythe placed its tank and field gun in the Grove by the Royal Military Canal, and even its eastern suburb of Seabrook received its own field gun.

Ashford's tank, one of only three left of its kind and the only one that remains in the place where it was presented, was given to the town on 1 August 1919. The Vickers Mark IV No. 245 was driven from the station yard as part of a grand procession headed by a band. At 3.7mph it was propelled up Station Road into the High Street before negotiating the tight corner of Castle Street into St George's

Square, where it can still be seen. The tank was accepted by Mr Kither, Chairman of Ashford Borough Council, and then savings certificates were offered for sale, with each purchaser allowed to view the inside of the tank. The day was rounded off with an evening's entertainment for the tank crew including dinner and a concert.

A search for the last resting place of Ashford's one air-raid victim, Gladys Sparkes, was sadly unsuccessful, as was a trip out to the lonely Isle of Grain to find little Ida Barden, so unluckily killed by a piece of the *Princess Irene* when it exploded in the Medway. Yet in the peaceful cemeteries of Folkestone, Dover, Margate, Ramsgate and the other air-raid towns, the innocent victims of war may be easily be found. Some of their memorials stand proudly amongst well-manicured lawns, while others hide shyly beneath a covering of stinging nettles and brambles in a hidden corner.

The Ashford tank crawls through the High Street on 1 August 1919. Marlinova Collection

Folkestone's many victims were mainly buried close to each other in Cheriton Road Cemetery by the railway line, and most of their headstones remain standing, though in varied states of preservation. Sadly, some of the inscriptions are no longer legible and the deceased lie forgotten and forsaken by those who came after them. Some of the dead lie in undisturbed country churchyards, wonderful places for quiet contemplation and a million miles away from the carnage of the days the Germans came. Some towns, such as Margate and Sheerness, commendably included their civilian dead on their war memorials, though, unhappily, for the town that suffered the greatest loss of all, Folkestone, this was not the case when its fine war memorial was erected at the top of the Road of Remembrance in 1922. The townsfolk instead had to accept a small plaque placed on the lamp-post outside Stokes's shop with the inscription, 'This tablet marks the place where on May 25th 1917 a bomb was dropped from a German plane killing 60 persons and injuring many others.' The 60 total, however, is one out; the death of Marie Snoawert on 26 June 1917 from injuries received in the raid seemingly having been excluded. Up until the commencement of the Second World War the Salvation Army held an annual memorial service at the plaque on the date of the disaster. The shop itself, which had been rebuilt and reopened within a month of the raid, was demolished after a fire in 1985 (the arsonist perished in the blaze) and the site was grassed over and left as a memorial

The site of Stokes's shop, Tontine Street, Folkestone today, showing the memorial plaque where 61 people were killed by a single bomb on 25 May 1917. Marlinova Collection

to those who had died, with the plaque being relocated onto the grass. In 2002 the adjoining Brewery Tap pub laid out a beer garden over the site and the plaque was relocated once again, onto the footpath.

As regards the other main Folkestone Gotha bomb-sites, Nos. 19 and 21 Bouverie Road East were rebuilt after the raid and survived until 2001, when they were demolished as part of a proposed shopping development. The bombed houses in St John's Street were patched up and remain to this day, but the Osborne Hotel appears not to have survived the Second World War. The remains of the totally wrecked 21 Manor Road were demolished and the site remained empty until a new property was erected in 1930 to house the Vicar of Christ Church (now Holy Trinity with Christ Church, the latter having been largely destroyed by a shell on 17 May 1942).

On 3 February 1932 a bomb from the Gotha raid (presumably a dud and not previously recorded) was found in the back garden of 24 St John's Street, from where it was taken to Dover and destroyed.

For those who had experienced the trauma of the raids and survived, the mental scars would remain indelible for the rest of their lives. Others were left with physical scars as a permanent reminder for all to see, such as Nellie Bowbrick, whose two daughters were killed in the Folkestone raid. The raid left her paralysed from the waist down after suffering compound fractures to the right leg, numerous shrapnel wounds and a very bad bruise to her back, and she was to remain in the Royal Victoria Hospital for nearly eight years. However, she dealt with her injuries with great fortitude and became quite a celebrity within the hospital. On 27 July 1921 Nellie was wheeled in her bed out to the car park to meet HRH the Prince of Wales, who had laid the foundation stone for the new nurses' home. She finally passed away on 24 March 1925 from heart failure due to sepsis from wounds suffered in the air raid. Mr G W Haines, the Borough Coroner, neatly summed up the feelings of many with the words: 'After a lapse of seven years we are bringing down the curtain on

Sheerness war memorial, pictured here shortly after its unveiling on 29 April 1922. As well as honouring the military dead, its civilian casualties are also listed, as are the military and civilian dead from the Bulwark *and* Princess Irene *explosions.* Marlinova Collection

A Zeppelin returns to Margate, but in more peaceful times, as it passes over Sweyn Road on 26 April 1930. Marlinova Collection

our wounds and sorrows. May those who were spared not be unmindful.'

And what of Adolf Genth, who for the love of his country assisted in bringing a foreign war home to the British people for the first time with such devastating results. For a toughened soldier like Adolf it was hard to accept that the war was over. After the cessation of hostilities on the Western Front he moved to protect Germany's vulnerable eastern frontier from Polish and Russian sorties for which the defeated and weak former enemy was a tempting morsel, and flew with the

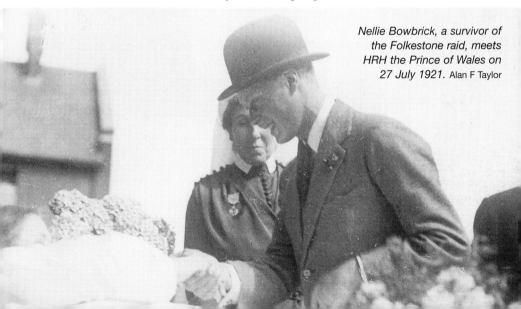

Nellie Bowbrick, a survivor of the Folkestone raid, meets HRH the Prince of Wales on 27 July 1921. Alan F Taylor

Adolf Genth in 1939, once again a soldier. He is wearing his First World War medals and his observer's badge. Thomas Genth

Artilleriefliegerstaffel 120 at Lyck in East Prussia. After a series of plebiscites were arranged to decide the German-Polish border Adolf became a demobilization officer at Neu Ruppin Airfield, where aircraft and other war materiel were broken up under the terms of the Treaty of Versailles. In September 1919 he finally left the army (in which he had spent 14 of his 25 years) and tried to eke out a civil life in what were very hard times for his country by becoming the manager of a seafreight company. He then turned his skills to weaving machinery and became manager of a company at Naumburg. In the meantime he also married, and fathered two sons. After a spell managing a branch in Greece he returned to Germany in 1928 and founded his own company.

Yet Adolf's strong sense of patriotism and feeling that Germany had been mistreated at Versailles led him, amongst many others, to rejoin a resurgent German army in 1934. He became a military pilot, continued his education as an observer and went to the *Luftkriegsakademie* Berlin-Gatow. In 1937 he became an officer in the German *Generalstab* and then graduated to chief of the IV. *Fliegerkorps* in 1939, the year that once again his country found itself at war with the old enemy Britain. However, on 10 January 1940, two Luftwaffe officers departing from the Münster-Loddenheide Airfield with top-secret plans of the proposed attack in the west were forced to land near Vucht in Belgium and the Belgians captured the plans. Adolf was declared responsible and was sent to the Front becoming commander of the III KG 76, based at Cormeilles-en-Vexin in France, from where bombers targeted Britain. Some 22 years after the Gotha raids Adolf found himself waging war once again over Britain, this time in the rather more sophisticated Dorniers. However, this time he was not to safely see the war through, for on 29 July 1940 his plane was attacked by the Hurricane of Flying Officer Patrick Woods-Scawen and Adolf was hit in the skull. The plane made it back, but Adolf died the same day and was laid to rest in Naumburg.

Adolf Genth (centre) pictured with his crew in front of a Dornier 17z c. 1940.
Thomas Genth

The funeral of Adolf Genth at Naumburg. The boy standing on the left is Thomas's father, aged 16, and the younger boy with the light suit is his brother Helmut, who was killed on the Eastern Front in 1945 at the age of 17 and whose body is still missing.
Thomas Genth

Thomas Genth says of his grandfather:

I am always asking myself what was my grandfather feeling when he flew to England in two world wars, in two different aeroplanes but with the same objective. Unfortunately it was never possible for me to talk to him and listen to his view of things. Yet surely it is only right that, as with the unfortunate civilian victims of war, he too should be remembered; as a patriot who died for his country.

Though it is perhaps understandable that in some people's eyes a tragic event such as the Folkestone raid should not be dwelt upon, it is rather sad that we alone should place flowers at the memorial plaque in Tontine Street each 25 May at 6.22 pm. Therefore hopefully this book will serve to bring the raid to the attention of a greater number of people and prove to be a suitable memorial, not only to those whose lives were taken away on that sunny May day, but to every First World War victim on both sides. Time really is a great healer.

The grave of Adolf Genth featuring the family coat of arms, a dog sitting on top of a helmet. Thomas Genth

A close-up view Folkestone's Tontine Street memorial plaque, showing its inscription.
Marlinova Collection

A Glint in the Sky

For Florrie and all the others

Calm spring evening look up high
See the glint in the sky
Grab the kids and see it through
Go and join the potato queue

Crashing sounds are getting near
But surely there is nothing to fear
Those Zeps it's said have had their day
We've gone and blown them all away

Anyway, Germans, no surely not
They promised not to bomb us lot
We fished their boys out from the deep
And in Cheriton Road they lie asleep

Busy in thought inside the store
Florrie stares patiently at the door
Soon it'll be time for walking home
Via viaduct and gas holder dome

And as the children continue to play outside
Their mothers begin to nervously hide
Except for those queuing at Stokes's shop
Upon whom the roof comes crashing down on top

Now ninety long years have since flown
The prayers have faded on their stones
And for them we can only stand and weep
As in Cheriton Road they lie asleep

MARTIN EASDOWN, 2004

Bibliography and Sources

PRIMARY SOURCES

Folkestone Herald
Folkestone Express
Hythe Reporter
East Kent Times
Isle of Thanet Gazette
Kent Messenger
Kentish Express
Ashford News
Dover Express and East Kent News
The Guardian and East Kent Advertiser
Scarborough Pictorial
Kelly's Directory of Folkestone 1916
The 1901 census for England and Wales
Folkestone Corporation minutes 1917
The Public Record Office, various documents
Imperial War Museum x22062/2
Home Forces GHQ Air Raids 1914-16
Imperial War Museum 97/3/1 The diary of Mrs A Purbrook
Imperial War Museum 94/2/1 The diary of Mrs L Peile
The Commonwealth War Graves Commission (www.cwgc.org.uk)

SECONDARY SOURCES

Aschoff, Walter. Londonflüge 1917 (Ludwig Voggenreiter Verlag 1940)
Baldwin, Ronald A. The Gillingham Chronicles (Baggins Book Bazaar 1998)
Bavington Jones, O G. Dover and the War (Dover Express c.1919)
Carlile, J C. Folkestone During the War 1914-1919 (F J Parsons 1920)
Castle, H G. Fire over England: The German Air Raids in World War I (Leo Cooper 1982)
Cole, Christopher and E F Cheesman. The Air Defence of Britain 1914-1918 (Putnam 1984)
Collyer, David. Flying: The First World War in Kent (North Kent Books 1982)
Coxon, Lieutenant Commander Stanley W. Dover During the Dark Days (John Lane 1919)
Easdown, Martin and Linda Sage. Rain, Wreck & Ruin: Disaster & Misfortune in Folkestone, Sandgate, Seabrook & Cheriton (Marlin Publications 1997)

Fegan, Thomas. The Baby Killers: German Air Raids on Britain in the First World War (Pen & Sword 2002)
Firth, J B. Dover and the Great War (Alfred Leney and Co. Ltd c.1920)
Filmer, Richard. Ashford in Old Picture Postcards (European Library 1987)
Franks, Norman, Frank Bailey and Rick Duiven. Casualties of the German Air Service 1914-1920 (Grub Street 1999)
Fredette, Raymond H. The First Battle of Britain (Cassell 1966)
Haddow G W and Peter M Grosz. The German Giants: The German R-Planes 1914-1918 (Putnam & Company Ltd. 1962)
Hook, John. This Dear Dear Land: Air Raids & Bombardments on Dover 1914-1918 (author 1994)
Hyde, Andrew P. The First Blitz: The German Air Campaign against Britain 1917-18 (Pen & Sword 2002)
Jones, John. Folkestone and the War (author 1919)
McCudden VC, Captain James. Flying Fury: Five Years in the Royal Flying Corps (Greenhill Books 2000)
MacDougall, Philip. The Hoo Peninsula (John Hallewell Publications 1980)
Marsay, Mark. Bombardment! The Day the East Coast Bled (Great Northern Publishing 1999)
Miller, Frederick. Under Shell Fire: The Hartlepools, Scarborough & Whitby under German Shell Fire (author 1915)
Moore, W G. Early Bird (Putnam 1963)
Morris, Joseph. German Air Raids on Britain 1914-1918 (The Naval & Military Press 1993, originally published in 1925 by Sampson Low, Marston & Co.)
Mould, David. Remember Scarborough 1914 (Hendon Publishing Co. 1978)
Ogley, Bob. Kent: A Chronicle of the Century Volume One 1900-1924 (Froglets Publications 1996)
Percival, Arthur. The Great Explosion at Faversham 2 April 1916 (reprinted from 'Archaeologia Cantiana' Vol. C, 1985)

Poolman, Kenneth. Zeppelins over England (Evans Brothers Limited 1960)
Rimell, Raymond L. Air War over Great Britain 1914-1918 (Arms and Armour Press Ltd 1987)
Rimell, Raymond Laurence. Zeppelin! A Battle for Air Supremacy in World War I (Conway Maritime Press 1984)
Rudkin, Mabel S. Inside Dover 1914-1918: A Woman's Impression (Elliot Stock 1933)
Von Eberhardt, Walter. Unsere Luftstreitkräfte 1914-1918 (Vaterländischer Verlagweller 1930)
White, C M. The Gotha Summer: The German Daytime Air Raids on England May-August 1917 (Robert Hale 1986)
Ramsgate During the Great War 1914-1918: A Souvenir of the Most Raided Part of England (A H Siminson 1919)
The War Zone in England: Thanet 1914-1918 (Tomson and Wotton 1919)
The German Raid on Whitby December 16th 1914 (Abbey Press 1915)
The German Raid on Scarborough December 16th 1914 (ETW Dennis and Sons Ltd 1915)
A German Crime: Bombardment of Scarborough December 16th 1914 (Scarborough Mercury Co. Ltd 1915)
Memorial of the German East Coast Raids and Bombardment by Sea and Air (Hood & Co. Ltd 1915)
Bygone Kent (various issues)
The Gotha GIV – The Englandflieger by Thomas Genth (www.angelfire.com)
The Great Folkestone Air Raid Friday 25th May 1917 by Janice Brooker (www.ancestry.com)
Sittingbourne Remembers: Zeppelins over Milton (www.pigstrough.co.uk)
In Memory of O A Jenner (www.fallenheroes.co.uk)
Gotha GIV (www.pilots-n-planes-ww1.com)
Zeppelins (www.constable.ca/zeppelin.htm)
www.theaerodrome.com

Index